Evangelical Anglicans

Evangelical Anglicans

Their Role and Influence in the Church Today

Edited by
R. T. France and A. E. McGrath

First published in Great Britain 1993
Society for Promoting Christian Knowledge
Holy Trinity Church
Marylebone Road
London NW1 4DU

British Library Cataloguing-in-Publication Data

A catalogue record for this book is available
from the British Library

ISBN 0-281-04661-1

Typeset by Pioneer Associates, Perthshire
Printed in Great Britain by
Mackays of Chatham plc, Chatham, Kent

Contents

Contents

The Contributors

Revd Dr Richard France is Principal of Wycliffe Hall, and lectures in New Testament. He was formerly a lecturer at the University of Ife and Ahmadu Bello University, Nigeria, and Warden of Tyndale House, Cambridge.

Revd Dr Alister McGrath is lecturer in historical and systematic theology at Wycliffe Hall. He was Bampton Lecturer at Oxford University in 1990.

Revd Dr David Atkinson is Fellow and chaplain of Corpus Christi College, Oxford and lectures in pastoral theology at Wycliffe Hall. He takes up the position of Chancellor of Southwark Cathedral in May 1993.

Revd Dr Nigel Biggar is chaplain of Oriel College, Oxford, and lectures on ethics at Wycliffe Hall.

Donald Hay is Fellow of Jesus College, Oxford, and lecturer in economics at the University of Oxford. He is a former member of Wycliffe Hall Council.

Revd Gerald Hegarty is lecturer in theology and spirituality at Wycliffe Hall and chaplain of St Edmund Hall, Oxford.

Most Revd Richard Holloway is Bishop of Edinburgh and Primus of the Scottish Episcopal Church. He was formerly vicar of St Mary Magdalen, Oxford.

Dr Gordon McConville is lecturer in Old Testament at Wycliffe Hall. He was previously on the staff of Trinity College, Bristol.

Revd Dr Oliver O'Donovan is Regius Professor of Moral and Pastoral Theology at Oxford University. A former student and member of staff of Wycliffe Hall, he is currently a member of Wycliffe Hall Council.

The Contributors

Revd Vera Sinton is Director of Pastoral Studies at Wycliffe Hall, and also lectures in ethics. She was previously on the staff of All Nations Christian College.

Revd Peter Southwell is Senior Tutor and lecturer in Old Testament at Wycliffe Hall, and chaplain of the Queen's College, Oxford.

Revd Gillian Sumner, a former student and until recently a member of staff at Wycliffe Hall, is Associate Principal of the Oxford Ministry Course, and a member of the General Synod.

Revd Graham Tomlin, a former student of the Hall, is lecturer in church history at Wycliffe Hall, and chaplain of Jesus College, Oxford.

Revd Dr David Wenham is lecturer in New Testament at Wycliffe Hall. He was previously lecturer in New Testament at Union Biblical Seminary, India, and Director of the Tyndale House Gospels Project, Cambridge.

Introduction

R. T. FRANCE and ALISTER McGRATH

Survey after survey demonstrates the same finding: evangelicalism is of growing importance to the worldwide church. Scarcely any part of the world has remained untouched by the global renaissance of evangelicalism. Even Latin America, traditionally regarded as a stronghold of Roman Catholicism, is now expected to become dominated by evangelicalism by the year 2025. The Anglican churches, and the Church of England in particular, are no exception to this rule. Anglicanism has been deeply affected, especially during the last two decades, by a resurgent evangelicalism within its ranks.

This naturally raises a fundamental question. How do evangelicalism and Anglicanism relate to each other? Are they in competition? Is it a mere marriage of convenience? How can they mutually enrich one another? What contributions can evangelicalism make to the life of the Anglican churches as the second millennium draws to its end? These questions are often asked, not least within the six evangelical theological colleges of the Church of England, responsible for more than half of the ordinands now in full-time training for ministry in that church.

It therefore seemed a good idea to bring together a group of writers associated with one such college, as an illustration of the kind of thinking that is going on within evangelical Anglicanism today. The contributors to this volume (except for Richard Holloway) are past or present members of either the teaching staff or the Council of Wycliffe Hall, Oxford. With the exception of Gordon McConville (a Presbyterian who worships at a local Anglican church), all are evangelical Anglicans. We have no doubt that contributions of equal quality could have been forthcoming from other evangelical theological colleges; there is, however, a

1

natural unity and affinity amongst the group of writers brought together in this volume, who share a common commitment to and vision for theological education and spiritual renewal within the Church of England.

Wycliffe Hall in itself stands as a symbol of the new confidence within evangelical Anglicanism, and the opportunities and challenges which it affords. Five of its nine members of staff and two of its four visiting lecturers are members of the Oxford University Faculty of Theology and make an active contribution towards the teaching of theology in the university. Five of the contributors are college chaplains, engaged in pastoral care within university communities, and committed to the belief that theology is and should be of pastoral relevance, rather than a mere subject for academic study. Yet the Hall is deeply committed to encouraging and promoting theological study and research within Oxford and the international academic community; in the last academic year (1991–2) seventeen nationalities were represented within the student body. Members of the Hall's staff frequently lecture and teach at theological institutions throughout the world, and we welcome the vision and stimulus brought to the Hall by overseas students and visitors. It is our hope that the contributions to this volume may be of service to both Anglicanism and evangelicalism throughout the world, although we note especially the affinity between the situations in England and those in Canada and Australasia.

The mood of these essays is a settled confidence, reflecting the sense of belonging and purpose which is becoming increasingly typical of evangelical Anglicanism today. Yet all is not well. We are also aware of deficiencies and weaknesses. Evangelicalism has yet to reach maturity. There are strong parallels with the Oxford movement of the 1830s: this attempt to renew the church and rediscover its catholic character probably took two generations to establish itself as a credible and serious force within the Church of England, undergoing much critical self-examination in doing so. Evangelical Anglicans are now going through much the same process of reflection and self-criticism. The reader will overhear some of these discussions in the course of the contributions to this volume. However, it is not only evangelicals who have the right to comment on such developments. For this reason, we have invited

2

a leading and widely respected Anglican Catholic, Richard Holloway, Bishop of Edinburgh, to provide a much-needed outside perspective on evangelical Anglicanism. His criticisms, which are here presented without any editorial alterations, will provide much food for thought for evangelicalism as it contemplates the future.

The shape of evangelicalism

The term 'evangelical' dates from the sixteenth century, when it was used to refer to catholic writers wishing to revert to more biblical beliefs and practices than those associated with the late medieval church. It was used especially in the 1520s, when the terms *évangélique* and *evangelisch* came to feature prominently in polemical writings of the early Reformation. In the 1530s the term 'Protestant' came to be more significant. However, this term was imposed upon evangelicals by their opponents, and was not one of their own choosing. 'Evangelical' is the term chosen by evangelicals to refer to themselves.

Evangelicalism may be said to centre upon a cluster of four assumptions. Historically, these have been:

1. The authority and sufficiency of Scripture.
2. The uniqueness of redemption through the death of Christ upon the cross.
3. The need for personal conversion.
4. The necessity, propriety and urgency of evangelism.

Other matters have tended to be regarded as *adiaphora*, 'matters of indifference', upon which a substantial degree of pluralism may be accepted.

Of particular importance is the question of ecclesiology. Historically, evangelicalism has never been committed to any particular theory of the church, regarding the New Testament as being open to a number of interpretations in this respect, and treating denominational distinctives as of secondary importance to the gospel itself. This most emphatically does *not* mean that evangelicals lack commitment to the church, as the body of Christ; rather, it means that evangelicals are not committed to any one *theory* of the church. A corporate conception of the Christian life is not understood to be specifically linked with any one denominational understanding of the nature of the church. In one sense, this is a 'minimalist' ecclesiology; in another, it represents an admission that the New Testament itself does not stipulate with precision any single form of church government, which can be made binding upon all Christians. This has had several major consequences, which are of central importance to an informed understanding of the movement.

First, evangelicalism is *transdenominational*. It is not confined to any one denomination, nor is it a denomination in its own right. There is no inconsistency involved in speaking of 'Anglican evangelicals', 'Presbyterian evangelicals', 'Methodist evangelicals', or even 'Roman Catholic evangelicals'. In the United States in particular, evangelicalism is becoming a significant force within the Roman Catholic church, with local Bible Study groups being the centre of renewal and growth. There is considerable cross-fertilization between leading evangelical institutions worldwide (many of which do not operate within denominational boundaries), especially seminaries, graduate schools of theology and research institutes, publishing houses, journals, television and radio networks, and ministerial conventions.

This has had the effect of making Anglican evangelicalism of enormous importance worldwide, with writers such as John Stott, James Packer and Michael Green having an influence which transcends Anglicanism, and reaches deep into Presbyterian, Baptist, Methodist, Lutheran, Reformed and other denominational circles throughout the English-speaking world and beyond. Liberal and Catholic traditions and writers within the Church of England frequently have no comparable transdenominational or international recognition, and their contribution can sometimes be seen as restricted, not merely to an Anglican, but to a narrowly *English* Anglican, agenda.

Secondly, evangelicalism is not a denomination in itself, possessed of a distinctive ecclesiology, but is a *trend within the mainstream denominations*. In the case of Anglicanism, the confrontation between John Stott and Martyn Lloyd-Jones at the Second National Assembly of Evangelicals on the evening of 18 October 1966 is of historic significance in this respect. Lloyd-Jones issued a passionate call for evangelicals within the mainstream churches to 'come out', and, in effect, form a denomination of their own. Stott insisted that their rightful place was within those mainstream denominations, which they could renew from within. The convening of the National Evangelical Anglican Congress at Keele University shortly afterwards (4–7 April 1967) sealed this development, and marks the beginning of the more positive role of evangelicalism within the Church of England, and the end of any serious 'separationist' party within English evangelicalism.

Thirdly, evangelicalism itself represents an *ecumenical* movement. There is a natural affinity amongst evangelicals, irrespective of their denominational associations, which arises from a common commitment to a set of shared beliefs and outlooks. The characteristic evangelical refusal to allow any specific ecclesiology to be seen as normative, while honouring those which are clearly grounded in the New Testament and Christian tradition, means that the potentially divisive matters of church ordering and government are treated as of secondary importance.

Fundamentalism and evangelicalism

An essential question which demands clarification at this point concerns the relation between fundamentalism and evangelicalism. At the semi-popular level, the discussion of this question in Britain has been, perhaps unfortunately, focused especially on James Barr's *Fundamentalism*, published in 1977. This vigorously polemical work was received with delight by those who disliked evangelicalism, intense irritation by evangelicals (who felt that they were all being tarred with the same indiscriminate brush), and with some scepticism by historians and sociologists, who noted its failure to make the crucial distinctions necessary to gain an understanding of fundamentalism, in its proper sense. For further comments on Barr's book see chapter 4 below.

In order to understand the essential differences between these two movements it is necessary to turn to the North American situation and the careful analysis of the relation between fundamentalism and evangelicalism presented by leading (non-evangelical) historians of American religion, most notably George

Marsden (Duke University) and Martin E. Marty (University of Chicago). Fundamentalism arose as a religious reaction within American culture to the rise of a secular culture.[1] It was from its outset, and has remained, a counter-cultural movement, using central doctrinal affirmations as a means of defining cultural boundaries. Certain central doctrines (most notably, the absolute literal authority of Scripture and the premillennial return of Christ) were treated as barriers, intended as much to alienate secular culture as to give fundamentalists a sense of identity and purpose. A siege mentality became characteristic of the movement; fundamentalist counter-communities viewed themselves as walled cities, or (to evoke the pioneer spirit) circles of wagons, defending their distinctives against an unbelieving culture.[2]

The emphasis upon the premillenial return of Christ is of especial significance. This view has a long history, but never attained any especial degree of significance prior to the nineteenth century. However, fundamentalism appears to have discerned in the idea an important weapon against the liberal Christian idea of a kingdom of God upon earth, to be achieved through social action. 'Dispensationalism', especially of a premillennarian type, became an integral element of fundamentalism. Such dispensationalist views, it must be stressed, have had far less impact within English evangelicalism of any shape during the twentieth century, least of all upon Anglican evangelicalism.

Yet disquiet became obvious within American fundamentalism during the late 1940s and early 1950s. 'Neo-evangelicalism' (as it has come to be known) began to emerge, committed to redressing the unacceptable situation created by the rise of fundamentalism. Within the specifically English context, fundamentalism and evangelicalism may now be distinguished at three levels.

First, *biblically*, fundamentalism is hostile to the notion of biblical criticism, in any form, and is committed to a literal interpretation of Scripture. Evangelicalism accepts the principle of biblical criticism (although insisting that this be used responsibly), and recognizes the diversity of literary forms within Scripture.[3] The massive development of evangelical biblical scholarship since 1977, surveyed briefly in this volume by Gordon McConville and R. T. France, and its growing acceptance within the international academic community, is a forceful witness to this point.

Second, *theologically*, fundamentalism is committed to a narrow set of doctrines, some of which evangelicalism regards as at best peripheral (such as those specifically linked with dispensationalism), and at worst an irrelevance. There is an overlap of beliefs (such as the *authority* of Scripture), which can too easily mask profound differences in outlook and temperament.

Third, *sociologically*, fundamentalism is a reactionary counter-cultural movement, with tight criteria of membership, and is often especially associated with a 'bluecollar' constituency. Evangelicalism is a cultural movement with increasingly loose criteria of self-definition, which tends to be more associated with a professional or 'whitecollar' constituency. The element of irrationalism often associated with fundamentalism is lacking in evangelicalism, which has produced significant writings in areas of the philosophy of religion and apologetics. The strong representation of evangelicalism within the student bodies of English universities, especially Oxford and Cambridge, should be noted here. The essays in this volume by Nigel Biggar and Donald Hay point to the commitment of evangelicals to social action and reflection within the English cultural situation, rather than — as in the case of fundamentalism — in isolation from it.

The break between fundamentalism and neo-evangelicalism in the late 1940s and early 1950s changed both the nature and the public perception of the latter. Billy Graham, perhaps the most publicly visible representative of this new evangelical style, became a well-known figure in English society, and a role model for a younger generation of evangelical ordinands. The recognition in America of the new importance and public visibility of evangelicalism dates from the early 1970s. The crisis of confidence within American liberal Christianity in the 1960s was widely interpreted to signal the need for the emergence of a new and more publicly credible form of Christian belief.[4] In 1976, America woke up to find itself living in the 'Year of the Evangelical', with a born-again Christian (Jimmy Carter) as its President, and an unprecedented media interest in evangelicalism, linked with an increasing involvement on the part of evangelicalism in organized political action.[5] It also became increasingly clear that many American evangelicals found Anglicanism attractive, particularly on account

7

of its emphasis upon a fixed public liturgy and lectionary.[6] The perceived aggressive bias towards a liberal agenda on the part of the Episcopal Church in the United States has prevented it from benefiting fully from this development; the Church of England, with its tradition of tolerance and openness, has perhaps been the chief beneficiary.

For these developments could not pass unnoticed and unheeded in England. The result has been a changing attitude towards evangelicalism, with even the British quality press discovering that there is more to evangelicalism than merely the playing of guitars in church. A single episode will illustrate this changing mood within the Church of England. In 1957 John Stott led a student mission at the University of Durham. This provoked a hostile and ill-tempered attack from Michael Ramsey, then Bishop of Durham, who wrote scathingly of 'our English Fundamentalism' – referring to the views associated with John Stott. Thirty years later, it became clear that such wooden stereotypes now firmly belonged to the past; Robert Runcie, towards the end of his period as Primate, described this same John Stott as the greatest Anglican since William Temple. It is still sadly true, however, that some recent writers of an older generation still use the terms 'fundamentalist' and 'evangelical' interchangeably, to mean little more than 'someone committed to the authority of Scripture', in much the same way as right-wing politicians tend to elide, not entirely accidentally, Marxism and socialism, or early critics of the Oxford movement attempted to equate 'Tractarianism' with 'Roman Catholicism'. None of the contributors to this volume see themselves, or are thought of, as 'fundamentalists'; they are, nonetheless, committed to the supreme authority of Scripture in Christian thought and life. Those who find this paradoxical have much rethinking to do.

The charge that evangelicalism is anti-intellectual, found in a number of Michael Ramsey's writings in the late 1950s, is now widely regarded as outdated. Evangelicals are heavily represented, to the highest level, in British university faculties of theology. Perhaps evangelicals were once suspicious that theological scholarship might damage their faith; that outlook is not shared by the contributors to this book, who regard responsible theological scholarship as having a significant contribution to make to the corporate life of the church, as well as to the individual's life of faith. We recognize, of course, that not all academic theology is responsible and devoid of partisan bias: one member of Oxford University's Faculty of Theology remarked recently to one of the editors that his personal mission in life was 'to turn conservative evangelicals into liberal Protestants'!

But enough has been said by way of introduction. Our themes await us.

Notes

1. The definitive study remains George Marsden, *Fundamentalism and American Culture: The Shaping of Twentieth Century Evangelicalism 1870-1925* (New York: Oxford University Press, 1980).
2. Martin E. Marty, 'Fundamentalism as a Social Phenomenon', in George Marsden, ed., *Evangelicalism and Modern America* (Grand Rapids, MI: Eerdmans, 1984), pp. 56-70.
3. See Mark A. Noll, *Between Faith and Criticism: Evangelical Scholarship and the Bible in America* (San Francisco: Harper & Row, 1982).
4. Leonard E. Sweet, 'The 1960s: The Crises of Liberal Christianity and the Public Emergence of Evangelicalism', in Marsden, *Evangelicalism and Modern America*, pp. 29-45.
5. There is a massive literature: see, for example, Robert C. Liebman and Robert Wuhtnow, *The New Christian Right: Mobilization and Legitimation* (New York: Aldine Publishing, 1983); Richard Quebedeaux, *The Young Evangelicals* (New York: Harper & Row, 1974); Judith L. Blumhofer and Joel A. Carpenter, *Twentieth Century Evangelicalism: A Guide to the Sources* (New York: Garland Publishing, 1990).
6. See Robert E. Webber, *Evangelicals on the Canterbury Trail: Why Evangelicals are Attracted to the Liturgical Church* (Waco, TX: Word Publishing, 1985).

1

Evangelical Anglicanism:
A Contradiction in Terms?

ALISTER McGRATH

Evangelicalism is the most rapidly growing constituent element within modern Christianity. The same pattern can be discerned throughout the world, whether we consider the United States, Latin America, or the Far East: evangelicalism is on the move. England has not been isolated from this development. Just as the Church of England was deeply affected by the growth of liberalism, particularly in the United States, during the 1960s and 1970s, so it has felt the impact of the growing strength of evangelicalism worldwide. Many have welcomed this development. I think of an Anglican congregation in Canada who, ten years back, insisted that their new rector would be an evangelical: 'That way, we'll get some growth round here!'[1] Others, however, have been more disturbed by the new shifts, and have raised fundamental anxieties about whether 'evangelicalism' and 'Anglicanism' bear any inherent relation to one another. Those concerns are genuine, and need to be addressed. This essay is concerned to explore the place of evangelicalism within the Anglican churches.

The essentials of Anglicanism

The doctrinal fluidity of Anglicanism is the subject of comment, rather than debate. The social conditions of England during the sixteenth century, during which Anglicanism may be argued to have come into being, made extensive doctrinal formulations on the part of the nascent English reformed church undesirable. Faced with the considerable difficulty of achieving a religious settlement in the midst of the instability of the period, Elizabeth I had little stomach for the protracted theological debates which would have been the inevitable prelude to, and continuing outcome of, a detailed Confession of Faith. Her concern was for religious peace, rather than doctrinal precision.[2] The need for doctrinal definition of considerable precision was evident in the case of Germany during the 1550s and 1560s: the co-existence of Lutheran and Roman Catholic communities in contiguous areas of the region led to demands for public criteria of demarcation, by which the rival communities could be distinguished from one another – a pressure which increased still further with the establishment of Calvinism in the Palatinate in the 1560s.[3] No comparable situation existed in England. As Robert Morgan remarks, 'in a fairly monolithic Christian culture, cut off by sea from neighbouring states, when Roman Catholics and other nonconformists could be penalized and marginalized, it was possible to maintain a church's boundaries largely by a common liturgy and polity'.[4] The Thirty-Nine Articles (1571) are explicitly described as 'for the avoiding of diversity of opinions and for the establishing of consent touching true religion'. They are not, and were never intended to be, a confession of faith.

This is not to say that the Articles are a set-piece of studied ambiguity; they are, in fact, quite explicit at a number of points, especially when interpreted within their historical context, and especially in the light of the continuing threat posed to the Elizabethan Settlement by a revitalized Roman Catholicism and an increasingly militant Puritan wing within the English church itself. On the contrary, they are minimal in their specifications. The Articles do not commit the reformed English church to anything other than an affirmation of the main points of the catholic faith, allowing a considerable degree of freedom in relation to areas of potential division (evident in the nuanced discussion of the highly contentious issue of predestination in Article XVII). If Anglicanism possesses 'essentials', they are 'essentials' that are common to the whole church of God, of which Anglicanism is part. Anglicanism's distinctive features may be argued to lie in its application of the gospel to a specific historical situation – England, and subsequently the British colonies. Louis Weil states this point rather well:

The gospel in Anglicanism is, then, one facet in a vast mosaic. In its essentials, it corresponds to the gospel as it has been proclaimed and believed all over the world. Yet it is also characterized by its particularity as an experience of God's saving work in particular cultures, and is shaped by the insights and limitations of persons who were themselves seeking to live the gospel within a particular context.[5]

Anglicanism, in its foundational stages, was thus not committed to any set of doctrines which can be designated as 'distinctively and exclusively Anglican'. The development of such distinctive doctrines, especially as they relate to matters of ecclesiology, is to be dated from a later stage in Anglican history, and cannot be detached from the 'particular context' in which those developments took place. Historically, Anglicanism has encompassed within its ample girth a variety of theological positions, regarding itself as possessed of a comprehensiveness which prevents the exclusion of demonstrably Christian positions. The latter was viewed as a sectarian tendency, inappropriate for a national established church. As a result, views which could be labelled 'evangelical', 'liberal', 'rationalist' or 'catholic' have been found throughout Anglican history. Let us hear Louis Weil once more:

> In its document *For the Sake of the Kingdom*, the Inter-Anglican Theological and Doctrinal Commission speaks convincingly of the pluriformity of the church. The Anglican tradition has encompassed 'differing styles of piety, differing idioms in theology, and differing agendas for Christian witness and action'. This diversity has been difficult for some Anglicans, who have wanted to envision the church in a single mould of their own design. But the document suggests that the pluralism which has characterized Anglicanism is in fact the reality in which the whole church finds itself.[6]

The acknowledgement of such intra-Anglican pluriformity is of crucial importance, in that it cuts the ground from under crude attempts to prescribe 'the spirit of Anglicanism', and set it in tablets of stone. For any one party within Anglicanism to claim that it, and it alone, represents the 'spirit of Anglicanism' is little more than an act of arrogance, based on a conveniently superficial reading of Anglican history.

I have no intention of claiming that evangelicalism is the only authentic form of Anglicanism. My concern is simply to insist that evangelicalism is, historically and theologically, a legitimate and respectable option within Anglicanism. At no point is evangelicalism inconsistent with any of the Thirty-Nine Articles, the only document, apart from Scripture, the creeds and the Prayer Book, regarded as authoritative for Anglicans.[7] Indeed, evangelicalism's characteristic emphasis upon the sufficiency of Scripture can be argued to be embodied in Article VI, just as its views on the spiritual and pastoral authority of the priest are superbly stated in the ordinals.

Evangelicals and ecclesiologies

Some suggest that evangelicalism is devoid of a distinctively Anglican ecclesiology. In one sense, an important point is being made: evangelicalism is a worldwide transdenominational movement, which is able to co-exist within every major denomination in the Western church, including the Roman Catholic church. Evangelicalism is not locked into a purely Anglican constituency, in the manner in which, to many observers, Anglo-Catholicism appears to have become. A commitment to a corporate conception of the Christian life does not entail the explicit definition of a theology of the church. Precisely because evangelicalism has no defining or limiting ecclesiology, it can accommodate itself to virtually any form of church order – including that of Roman Catholicism.

This is well illustrated by the history of the movement. Evangelical attitudes are now known to have been deeply embedded within the Italian church during the 1520s and 1530s,[8] with prominent Italian church leaders (including several cardinals) meeting regularly in a number of cities to study Scripture and the writings of the Protestant reformers.[9] No tension was seen between an evangelical spirituality and a catholic ecclesiology; it was only when the situation was radically politicized in the 1540s through the intrusion of imperial politics into theological debate that evangelicalism came to be seen as a destabilizing influence within the Italian church. Similar developments are now known to be taking place within the Roman Catholic church in the United

States, as an increasing number of members find evangelicalism conducive to their spiritual needs – yet do not feel (and are not *made* to feel) that their espousal of an evangelical spirituality entails abandoning their loyalty to Catholic church structures.

Yet a fundamental question must be raised here. Does Anglicanism really have a distinctive theology of the church? The Elizabethan Settlement of 1559, dominated by pragmatic considerations, set up an established national episcopal church without feeling the need to justify such a step on theological grounds. That such ecclesiologies were developed by later writers, such as the Caroline divines, is unquestionable; it is equally beyond dispute that some Anglicans have accepted them. But are they binding? As John Selden (1584–1654) reminds us, such theologians have no corporate authority: 'The way is to consult the liturgies, not any private man's writing. As if you would know how the Church of England serves God, go to the Common-Prayer-Book, consult not this nor that man.'[10] That Book of Common Prayer commits Anglicans to nothing more than a minimalist ecclesiology and the three-fold ministry of bishops, priests and deacons, which Anglican evangelicals can happily embrace. It is currently fashionable to speak of evangelicals having an 'under-developed ecclesiology'; perhaps it might be suggested that it is others who have over-developed ecclesiologies? This is not to challenge their right to develop such ecclesiologies, and find in them much that is helpful. It is, however, to challenge their right to impose those ecclesiologies upon others, and declare that such theories, and such theories alone, are 'Anglican'. All may accept them; some do accept them; none must accept them.

Evangelicalism as a threat to Anglicanism?

Inevitably, evangelicalism's rapid expansion in the last two decades has raised considerable anxieties for many within Anglicanism, especially those with a more catholic outlook. Might not Anglicanism lose its distinctive identity as a result of this development? Ought not preservation measures – such as restricting the number of evangelical ordinands, or ensuring minimal evangelical representation on church bodies (including ministerial training courses) – be adopted, to restrict such a development?

(Many evangelicals suspect, not entirely without reason, that such developments are already taking place, and look forward to the day when evangelicalism is properly represented within the formal structures of the church.)

Yet the Church of England is a living body, rather than a petrified fossil which bears only the marks of the past and has lost any ability to grow and develop in response to present conditions. It is a dynamic body, which is open to renewal and revitalization as an essential part of its communal life and development. During the 1830s, many regarded the Oxford movement as an utterly un-Anglican development, which could only destroy the distinctiveness of the Church of England and move it closer to the Roman Catholic church. Its distinctive approach to worship was viewed with horror by some tender souls, who failed to appreciate that many ordinary parishioners genuinely found them to be helpful, and conducive to the praise and adoration of God. This intense suspicion remained for some time. Happily, the Oxford movement can now be seen for what it was – a renewing influence, bringing new life to the church and its worship.

Those same charges are today being brought by some less perceptive critics against evangelicals. Yet Anglican evangelicalism is a force for renewal within today's Church of England. As statistic after statistic reminds us, an English church which is growing today is most likely to be evangelical in its orientation. Those who are so culturally conditioned that they are unable to worship save with the assistance of a full pipe organ and robed choir will naturally deplore the more liberated style of worship often associated with evangelicalism, which has proved so attractive and helpful to many – especially young people – who would otherwise have nothing to do with the church. Future historians are likely to view today's critics of Anglican evangelicalism with as little sympathy as yesterday's critics of Anglo-Catholicism.

There is, however, a more serious point here. Evangelicalism is coming to dominate Christianity in the United States. Forms of American evangelicalism which are totally unsympathetic to the Anglican tradition are already establishing themselves in England. If their growth rate here bears any relation to that experienced elsewhere in the world (such as Latin America),[11] they will not

15

merely attract individuals who, potentially, could be Anglicans: they will draw people out of the Church of England into their own groups, severely weakening the presence and influence of our church in the nation. The presence of evangelicalism within the Church of England is a necessary check against this development, and ensures that the Church of England will, if anything, benefit from – rather than be seriously depleted and discredited by – the substantial growth in evangelicalism worldwide. Rather than deplore this growth in evangelicalism, those concerned for the future of Anglicanism would do better to encourage and nourish those evangelicals who are committed to Anglican outlooks and structures, thus ensuring that growth and renewal are channelled towards, rather than away from, the Church of England.

The evangelical affirmation of Anglicanism

In the past, evangelicals have been criticized for failing to be committed to the institutions and practices of Anglicanism as a whole. There is much truth in these criticisms. In the 1940s and 1950s, evangelicals chose to distance themselves from the mainstream of church life, perceiving themselves – as they in turn were perceived – to be outsiders. A siege mentality descended over the movement, expressed in an aggressiveness which ultimately rested upon a deep sense of insecurity and defensiveness. Their agenda was little more than that of survival, in a period in which the movement seemed set to be overwhelmed by the continuing strength of Anglo-Catholicism, an increasingly confident liberalism, and a new commitment to an ecumenical movement which regarded a concern for 'right doctrine' as a pointless archaism. The ill-informed, uncritical and totally unmerited identification of 'evangelicals' with 'fundamentalists' by Michael Ramsey (then Bishop of Durham, responding to a mission at Durham University by John Stott) poisoned the atmosphere within the evangelical constituency. Many evangelicals within the Church of England came to see their loyalties as lying with the separationist programme outlined and commended by Dr Martyn Lloyd-Jones in October 1966. Perhaps one of the most attractive features of Lloyd-Jones's vision of an evangelical denomination separated from the mainstream churches was the emphasis placed upon doctrinal purity – always a central concern of evangelicals.

16

Yet a change of mood was in the air in the early 1960s. Growing numerical strength within evangelicalism was accompanied by a heightened awareness of the detachment of the movement from the everyday life and concerns of the Church of England. As the attraction of the vision offered by Lloyd-Jones waned, the possibility of a revitalized evangelicalism which was committed to Anglican structures of ministry, worship and pastoral care began to emerge as a serious possibility. At the 1967 Islington Clerical Conference, the chairman addressed this possibility with a candour which would have been impossible a generation earlier:

> The Church of England is changing. Indeed, it is in a state of ferment – although it remains to be seen whether ferment will result in a mature vintage. On the other hand, Evangelicals in the Church of England are changing too. Not in doctrinal conviction (for the truth of the gospel cannot change), but (like any healthy child) in stature and posture. It is a tragic thing, however, that Evangelicals have a very poor image in the Church as a whole. We have acquired a reputation for narrow partisanship and obstructionism. We have to acknowledge this, and for the most part we have no one but ourselves to blame. We need to repent and to change. As for partisanship, I for one desire to be rid of all sinful 'party spirit'.

The National Evangelical Anglican Congress (affectionately known as NEAC), held at Keele University in April 1967, was a watershed, not merely in the history of English evangelicalism, but also in the history of the Church of England. 519 clergy and 481 laypersons chose to turn their backs on the isolationism of the past, and commit themselves to working within the Church of England. Although the charge of 'evangelical isolationism' is occasionally repeated in modern debates, that charge now belongs to an earlier generation.

Space permits only one illustration of this changed attitude. In his address to the Congress, Michael Green – then Senior Tutor at the London College of Divinity and, at thirty-six, the youngest speaker at the conference – spoke of the importance of Holy Communion, and pleaded for its reinstatement within evangelicalism.[12] His point was heard. Anglican evangelicals, who had hitherto tended to regard Morning and Evening Prayer as the only regular

17

services worthy of note, resolved not merely to reconsider this position, but to commit themselves to rediscover the centrality of Holy Communion:

> We have failed to do justice in our practice to the twin truths that the Lord's Supper is the main service of the people of God, and that the local church, as such, is the unit within which it is properly administered. This is not to undervalue in any way attendance at other services of the day, but to admit that we have let the sacrament be pushed to the outer fringes of church life and the ministry of the Word be divorced from it ... We determine to work towards the practice of a weekly celebration of the sacrament as the central corporate service of the church.[13]

As the contribution by Peter Southwell to this volume will make clear, the renewed valuing of the sacraments by evangelicals has proved to be no flash in the pan.

An unfinished agenda

Thus far, my concern has been to argue that evangelicalism has a proper place inside the Church of England, and that there is no inconsistency in speaking of 'Anglican evangelicals' or 'evangelical Anglicans'. For many, the suggestion that evangelicals are somehow 'un-Anglican' in any case belongs to yesteryear, reflecting the petty imperialism of Anglican party politics of a bygone period. But if part of my argument has been that Anglicanism ought to embrace evangelicalism, the remainder is that evangelicalism ought to embrace Anglicanism with greater fervour than has often hitherto been the case. I wish to note one point in particular, at which Anglicanism can offer evangelicalism important insights – the pastoral importance of an open church.

Let me illustrate this point from a discussion which has arisen within the evangelical community in Australia. In a highly charged article published in the April 1992 number of the leading Australian evangelical magazine, *On Being*, John Waterhouse argues that the evangelical movement may have lost its way, having accommodated itself too much to the spirit of secular culture.[14] Surveying the confusion within Australian evangelicalism, he comments:

The only winner is, paradoxically, the Anglican church. With its tradition of not precipitously separating the wheat from the tares, or pressuring people into public commitments before they are ready, the tentative outsider is given time to grow into faith, while the long-term believer, burnt out by a negative church experience, is given time to lick his wounds.[15]

A separatist view of the church – favoured by many non-Anglican evangelicals – carries with it the danger of imposing such doctrinal commitments upon church attendance that the mere attending of church can be seen as equivalent to a public Christian profession. The more Anglican tradition (which here corresponds to the Augustinian outlook of the mainstream Reformation) is that of assuming that the congregation will include both believers and unbelievers, and that attendance at church does not necessarily signify any profession of Christian faith.[16] Statistics suggest that one of the main routes by which people (especially over the age of thirty) come to faith is through attending church, and gradually assimilating, accepting and responding to the gospel. A separatist ecclesiology, with its emphasis upon commitment and doctrinal purity, makes this proven route to faith highly problematic.

Evangelicalism does not, as I have argued, possess a distinctive ecclesiology; at no point is an evangelical committed to or defined by a theory of the church. Evangelicals are thus at liberty to adopt any ecclesiology which is grounded in Scripture, lent dignity by the weight of Christian tradition, and consonant with pastoral wisdom. I wish to suggest that Anglicanism offers a vision of the church which evangelicals can and should embrace, which is consistent with the New Testament, grounded in the Christian tradition, and capable of functioning as a sound pastoral and evangelistic base. Too often, evangelical Anglicans have been hesitant over affirming their Anglicanism; surely the time has come to change this?

Conclusion

To conclude: I have argued that evangelicalism and Anglicanism are symbiotic, combining to provide an environment in which the inherent dynamism of evangelicalism can be harnessed and more effectively directed through the catholic structures of the Church of England. Recent studies of evangelicalism have suggested that the movement gains the ascendancy when mainstream Christianity is vulnerable and in decline;[17] that is the situation faced by our churches in Britain, Canada and Australasia. Evangelicalism may well prove to be a catalyst for revival and revitalization within Anglicanism, as Methodism once renewed the English church two centuries ago. Yet Anglicanism may also be the catalyst for the maturing and coming of age of evangelicalism. Despite its historical roots, evangelicalism is widely seen as the new kid on the ecclesiastical block. It needs to grow up, and learn the hard facts of life. Anglicanism can provide an environment for that maturing process. I believe that one needs the other, and hope that the years ahead will see them growing closer – and growing together.

Notes

1. The congregation subsequently grew from an average of 90 to an average of 450 on a Sunday morning.
2. See W. P. Haugaard, *Elizabeth and the Settlement of Religion* (Cambridge: Cambridge University Press, 1968); N. L. Jones, *Faith by Statute: Parliament and the Settlement of Religion* (London: Royal Historical Society, 1982).
3. See the outstanding study of Martin Heckel, 'Reichsrecht und "Zweite Reformation": Theologisch-juristische Probleme der reformierten Konfessionalisierung', in Heinz Schilling, ed., *Die reformierte Konfessionalisierung in Deutschland – Das Problem der 'Zweiten Reformation'* (Gütersloh: Gerd Mohn, 1986), pp. 11–43.
4. R. Morgan, ed., *The Religion of the Incarnation: Anglican Essays in Commemoration of Lux Mundi* (Bristol: Bristol Classical Press, 1989), p. xvi. The point is further discussed in Alister E. McGrath, 'Dogma und Gemeinde: Zur sozialen Funktion des christlichen Dogmas', *Kerygma und Dogma* 37 (1991), pp. 24–43.
5. Louis Weil, 'The Gospel in Anglicanism', in S. Sykes and J. Booty, eds, *The Study of Anglicanism* (London: SPCK, 1988), pp. 51–76; quote at p. 75.
6. Weil, 'Gospel in Anglicanism', p. 74.
7. To these, many would add the Anglican Ordinal.
8. See E. M. Jung, 'On the Nature of Evangelism in Sixteenth-Century Italy', *Journal of the History of Ideas* 14 (1953), pp. 511–27.
9. The subject is fascinating. For masterly surveys in English, see Barry Collett, *Italian Benedictine Scholars and the Reformation* (Oxford:

Clarendon Press, 1985); Dermot Fenlon, *Heresy and Obedience in Tridentine Italy* (Cambridge: Cambridge University Press, 1972).

10. John Selden, *Table-Talk* (London: William Pickering, 1847), p. 115.

11. See David Martin, *Tongues of Fire: The Explosion of Protestantism in Latin America* (Oxford: Blackwell, 1990).

12. Michael Green, 'Christ's Sacrifice and Ours: Relating Holy Communion to the Cross', in J. I. Packer, ed., *Guidelines: Anglican Evangelicals Face the Future* (London: Falcon Books, 1967), pp. 87–117.

13. *Keele '67: The National Evangelical Anglican Congress Statement* (London: CPAS, 1967), p. 35.

14. John Waterhouse, 'The Crisis of Evangelicalism', *On Being* 19/3, 1992, pp. 4–8.

15. Waterhouse, 'Crisis of Evangelicalism', p. 7.

16. For a comparison of evangelical ecclesiologies, see Robert C. Walton, 'A Mixed Body or a Gathered Church of Visible Saints: John Calvin and William Ames', in W. van't Spijken, ed., *Calvin: Erbe und Auftrag* (Kampen: Kok Pharos, 1991), pp. 168–78.

17. See John Stackhouse, 'The Emergence of a Fellowship: Canadian Evangelicalism in the Twentieth Century', *Church History* 60 (1991), pp. 247–62.

2
Evangelicalism and Biblical Authority

ALISTER McGRATH and DAVID WENHAM

The authority of the Word of God

At the centre of evangelicalism lies the belief that God has made himself known in and through Jesus Christ. This is not a specifically evangelical belief: it is the common heritage of the Christian church. Karl Barth is but one of the great theologians of the Christian church to affirm this point:

> When Holy Scripture speaks of God, it concentrates our attention and thoughts upon one single point and what is to be known at that point . . . And if we look closer, and ask: who and what is at this point upon which our attention and thoughts are concentrated, which we are to recognise as God, . . . then from its beginning to its end, the Bible directs us to the name of Jesus Christ.[1]

Michael Ramsey states precisely the same theological principle as Barth, even if his style is more Anglican: 'The importance of the confession "Jesus is Lord" is not only that Jesus is divine but that God is Christlike.'[2] If evangelicalism is distinctive at this point, it is on account of the emphasis it has chosen to place upon this belief, and the inferences which it draws from it, rather than the substance of the belief itself.

For evangelicals, Christology is primary; inevitably, however, it leads on to a belief in scriptural authority. In the first place, evangelicals observe that Jesus Christ himself saw Scripture (in his case, the Old Testament) as God-given. This conviction cannot be regarded as something he uncritically accepted from his

22

contemporaries; Christ had little hesitation in criticizing those beliefs and practices of Judaism which he regarded as unacceptable. Nor can it be treated as something that was incidental to his teaching; there are excellent reasons for asserting that it was integral to his own understanding of his mission, and a central component of his authoritative teaching.[3] Most Christians acknowledge that the teaching of Jesus possesses an inherent normative status; evangelicals insist that allegiance to Christ as Lord includes acceptance of his attitude to Scripture. Recently, John Barton has suggested that 'Christians are not those who believe in the Bible, but those who believe in Christ.'[4] While this has some merit as a statement of priorities and emphasis, it nevertheless sets up a misleading and unhelpful false dichotomy. It is not a question of *either* the Bible *or* Christ, as if they can or should be separated. There is an organic and essential connection between them. We honour Christ by receiving both the Scriptures which he received, and those which the church has handed down to us as a divinely inspired witness to Christ.

In the second place, and following on from what has just been said, Christology and scriptural authority are inextricably linked, in that it is Scripture which brings us to a knowledge of Jesus Christ. John Calvin correctly defined this as the whole point of Scripture.[5] The New Testament is the only document we possess which the Christian church has recognized as authentically embodying and recollecting its understanding of Jesus, and the impact which he had upon people's lives and thought. The reports we have concerning Jesus from extracanonical sources are of questionable reliability, and strictly limited value.[6] The same God who gave Jesus Christ also gave Scripture as a testimony to Christ. It is precisely through the written word of Scripture that we, who live after Christ, have access to the living Word of God, given in history.

The authority of Scripture thus rests upon both theological and historical considerations: it is through Jesus Christ that the distinctively Christian knowledge of God comes about, and this knowledge of Jesus is given only in Scripture. Christ is what gives Scripture its unity: as the missionary and Anglican statesman Bishop Stephen Neill, who spent his final years as scholar-in-residence at Wycliffe Hall, has emphasized, the central thought and subject which binds all parts of the Bible together, and in the light of which they are to be interpreted, is the person and work of Jesus Christ.[7]

The evangelical insistence upon the authority of Scripture reflects a determination not to permit anything from outside the Christian heritage to become the norm for what is truly 'Christian'. Recent theological history has provided us with examples of what happens when a theology cuts itself loose from the controlling influence of the Christian tradition, and seeks norms from outside that tradition – for example, in 'German culture'. Evangelicalism is grounded in the belief that Christianity must remain faithful to itself, by taking its heritage with the utmost seriousness, and refusing to be controlled by anything other than the living Christ, as we find him in Scripture. Evangelicals affirm, with the German Confessing Church at the time of the Third Reich, that:

> Jesus Christ, as he is attested for us in Holy Scripture, is the one Word of God which we have to hear and which we have to trust and obey in life and in death. We reject the false doctrine, as though the Church could and would have to acknowledge as a source of its proclamation, apart from and besides this one Word of God, still other events and powers, figures and truths, as God's revelation.[8]

In aligning itself with such declarations, evangelicalism affirms its intent to remain faithful to Jesus Christ, as he is made known through Scripture, and to avoid becoming enslaved to the 'self-images of the age' (Alasdair MacIntyre). To allow one's ideas and values to become controlled by anything or anyone other than the self-revelation of God in Scripture is to adopt an ideology, rather than a theology; it is to become controlled by ideas and values whose origins lie outside the Christian tradition – and potentially to become enslaved to them.

Such ideas and values may be powerful correctives to lazy and irresponsible theologies, just as Marxism has provided an overdue critique of Christian social thought and feminism of patriarchal tendencies within the church. But Marxist values and 'women's experience' – to name but two pertinent examples to which others could readily be added – cannot become *foundational* for Christianity, which is grounded in God, as he has made himself known in

24

Christ. Evangelicalism refuses to look anywhere else than Jesus Christ as the foundation of its faith, hope, worship and theology. The example of the German church under Hitler is instructive, in that it points to the need for a criterion by which the church can judge the secular world. A theology which is grounded in values drawn solely from the secular world, whether radical or conservative, becomes powerless to criticize that world. A theology grounded in German culture thus found itself powerless to criticize that culture; what was once believed to be liberating turned out to be decidedly sinister. It is significant that it was theologians such as Dietrich Bonhoeffer, who refused to look for God anywhere other than in Jesus Christ, who provided the most serious and thoughtful opposition to the Third Reich.

For evangelicals, the authority of Scripture is grounded both positively and negatively. It is grounded *positively*, in that God has chosen to make himself known to us. And that revelation finds its distinctively Christian focus and climax in the person of Jesus Christ. Yet it is also grounded *negatively*, in that there is no other reliable source of knowledge about God available. This point is too easily overlooked, and requires further attention.

Christianity talks about God. But which God? What is he, she or it – or *they*, for that matter – like? Underlying these questions, however, is a prior question: how do we discover what God is like in the first place? Where do we look to find out about God? A neutral observer, looking at the world and the human religious scene, might be forgiven for having doubts about whether we can know anything about God. The different religious traditions of humanity have come up with such radically different ideas that it is difficult to see anything in common between them.

Furthermore, the term 'religion' is itself far less well-defined than we might think. Underlying much recent Western liberal discussion of 'the religions' is a naive assumption that 'religion' is a genus, an agreed category, so that an appeal to 'religion' or 'religious experience' is a universally acceptable notion. In fact, it is nothing of the sort. In an important recent study, John Milbank stresses that the central 'assumption about a religious genus' does not even remotely amount to the 'recognition of an evident truth.'[9] 'Religion' has become a category which is largely imposed upon, rather than discerned within, human culture. We must therefore

25

be intensely suspicious of the Western assumption that 'religion' is a well-defined category, which can be neatly distinguished from 'culture' as a whole. Furthermore, the appeal to uninterpreted 'religious experience' as a starting point for theology has been subjected to serious criticism in recent years, particularly by the Yale theologian George Lindbeck.[10] 'Experience' turns out to be an ill-defined category, incapable of bearing the theological weight that many liberal writers would like to place upon it.

Others might suggest that unaided human reason can give us a reliable and thorough account of the nature and purposes of God. This viewpoint, characteristic of the Enlightenment, was persuasive in its own day. However, there has been a growing realization that reason has proved incapable of delivering what it seemed to promise. Alasdair MacIntyre makes this point as follows: 'The legacy of the Enlightenment has been the provision of an idea of rational justification which it has proved impossible to attain.'[11] The rise of postmodernism has still further undermined the notion of a 'rational theology'. Sadly, many who are openly critical of Scripture have yet to extend the same critical analysis to other theological resources – supremely reason, experience and 'religion'. The evangelical will insist, for critically informed reasons, that Scripture offers the most reliable knowledge of God available to the church, and concentrates it in the person and work of Jesus Christ.

Yet 'knowledge of Christ' embraces far more than the repetition of historical events; it includes, as an integral part of that knowledge, an *interpretation* of those events. Jesus Christ did not merely die; he died 'for our sins' (1 Cor. 15.3). As Wolfhart Pannenberg and others have emphasized, the scriptural narrative weaves together historical narrative and theological interpretation, making the isolation of 'history' and 'theology' virtually impossible, even if it were to be regarded as necessary. The complexity of the interaction of event and meaning has been well brought out by philosophers of history such as Raymond Aron, who wrote: 'The brute fact of the assassination [of Julius Caesar] would not interest anyone, unless it is put in its place within the totality brought about by the crisis of the Roman power, the resistance of the senatorial aristocracy to personal power, and so on.'[12] Similarly, the meaning of the crucifixion and resurrection depends upon their being seen within the totality of Old Testament messianic expectations and certain patterns of divine activity in history.

For this reason, among many others, the Old Testament continues to be of abiding significance for Christians, not only in that it bears witness to the continuing salvific action of God in history prior to the coming of Jesus Christ, but also in that it establishes the 'totality of context' within which the meaning of Christ's life, death and resurrection are to be interpreted. These events cannot be interpreted at random in an arbitrary framework of reference, or one chosen at will by a biased interpreter: Scripture itself bears witness both to the event and its proper interpretative framework.

There is also a pneumatological component to the evangelical understanding of biblical authority. The unique authority and status of Scripture rests upon the activity of the Holy Spirit, both in relation to the biblical material itself, and the subsequent process of interpretation and inward appropriation on the part of the reader. In neither case does the work of the Holy Spirit negate the work of the human agent. Inspiration is not dictation. There is a parallel here with the incarnation: Christ in his one person was both God and man; so Scripture is both divine and human. Just as Christ's divinity does not abrogate Christ's human nature, so the divine authorship of Scripture does not abolish its human authorship.[13] It is simply not true that evangelicalism denies the presence of a human element in Scripture, as some of its critics, more concerned to vilify than to understand, persist in maintaining. Evangelicalism rejoices in the presence of a human element in Scripture, as in Christ, and that God should have revealed himself in and through humanity in both these manners.

The centrality of Scripture to evangelical theology and spirituality rests upon considerations such as these. Yet this is not to say that evangelicalism is narrowly biblicist. Rightly understood, Scripture defines the centre of gravity of evangelicalism, not the limits of its reading or knowledge. Scripture is, for evangelicals, the central legitimating resource of Christian faith and theology, the clearest window through which the face of Christ may be seen. In seeing Scripture as the inspired, authoritative and trustworthy word of God, evangelicals are reiterating the common faith of the Christian church, not inventing something new. It was a leading

27

liberal Anglican writer, Alan Richardson, who stated: 'The Bible is and remains the appointed means of God's conversation with men.'[14] If evangelicalism is distinctive at this point, it is on account of the *emphasis* it has chosen to place upon this belief, rather than the substance of the belief itself.

The Word of God and the people of God

Across the Anglican churches, evangelical or not, liturgy, with its high component of biblical material, is what unites the people of God in their common worship. At the reading of the Old Testament or epistle at the Eucharist, the following words are used to conclude the reading, and indicate the seriousness with which it is to be received: 'This is the Word of the Lord'. John Barton laments the introduction of what he calls this 'dreadful formula' into recent Anglican liturgy.[15] We, however, welcome it, as a summary both of Scripture's view of itself (note especially 2 Tim. 3.15–16 and 2 Pet. 1.21), and of the manner in which Scripture has been understood and honoured within the Christian tradition. We agree that a simplistic interpretation of the phrase could be misleading; the words of Job's comforters, for example, are indeed part of the 'Word of the Lord', but not what the Lord (or the author of Job) wants us to believe.

But how do 'word' and 'people' relate? Evangelicals have always been prone to read Scripture as if they were the first to do so. The Anglican ethos provides an invaluable corrective to this tendency, by reminding us that others have been there before us, and have read it before us. This process of receiving the scriptural revelation is 'tradition' – not a source of revelation in addition to Scripture, but a particular way of understanding Scripture which the Christian church has recognized as responsible and reliable. Scripture and tradition are thus not to be seen as two alternative sources of revelation; rather they are coinherent. Scripture cannot be read as if it had never been read before. It is one of the great merits of Anglicanism that its liturgy constantly reminds us that Scripture has been read, valued and interpreted in the past. J. I. Packer, one of the most influential evangelical Anglican writers of recent years, stresses this point:

The Spirit has been active in the Church from the first, doing the work he was sent to do – guiding God's people into an understanding of revealed truth. The history of the Church's labour to understand the Bible forms a commentary on the Bible which we cannot despise or ignore without dishonouring the Holy Spirit. To treat the principle of biblical authority as a prohibition against reading and learning from the book of church history is not an evangelical, but an anabaptist mistake. [16]

'Tradition' is thus rightly understood (for example, by both the Reformers and the Second Vatican Council) as a history of discipleship – of reading, interpreting and wrestling with Scripture. Tradition is a willingness to read Scripture, taking into account the ways in which it has been read in the past. It is an awareness of the communal dimension of Christian faith, which calls the shallow individualism of many evangelicals into question. There is more to the interpretation of Scripture than any one individual can discern. It is a willingness to give full weight to the views of those who have gone before us in the faith. Once more, it is here that Anglicanism offers a vital and necessary check to evangelicalism, by providing forceful reminders – especially in and through the liturgy – of the corporate nature of the Christian faith, including the interpretation of Scripture.

At first sight, this emphasis on the importance of the community of faith might seem to be in tension with the belief that it is Scripture alone which is authoritative. But this principle was never intended by writers such as Luther or Calvin to mean that Scripture is to be read individualistically. It was not meant to elevate the private judgement of an individual above the communal judgement of the church (although it was interpreted in this way by certain radical reformers, outside the mainstream of the Reformation). Rather, it affirms that every traditional way of reading Scripture must, in principle, be open to challenge. As the study of church history makes clear, the church may sometimes get Scripture wrong: the sixteenth-century reformers believed that Scripture had been misunderstood at a series of junctures by the medieval church, and undertook to reform its practices and doctrines at those points. This, however, is a case of a tradition being criticized and renewed from within, in the light of the biblical foundations upon which it ultimately rests, and is recognized to rest. The Reformers did not regard themselves as founding a new tradition; their concern was to reform a tradition which already existed, but which appeared to have become detached from its scriptural foundations.

For in part, the authority of Scripture rests in the universal acceptance of that authority within the Christian church. In the case of Anglicanism, the church insists that Scripture shall be read and expounded as part of the corporate worship of the people of God. To recognize Scripture as authoritative is not the judgement of a group of individuals; it is the witness of the church down the ages. We trust the Bible partly because it is inherently worthy of trust, and partly because it is trusted by the church. In ascribing authority to Scripture, we are not merely recognizing and honouring God's decision to reveal himself to us, nor only the specific form which this took in Jesus Christ; we are also honouring a living tradition, which has remained faithful to the modes of faith and life made known and made possible through Jesus Christ, and mediated through Scripture. There is an organic connection between the Word of God and the people of God.

Biblical authority and biblical criticism

But what does the evangelical make of modern biblical criticism? How does an evangelical reconcile the view of Scripture as the Word of God with the views of the critics? The biblical critical movement has focused attention on the Bible as a human book written by human authors. It has asked, and attempted to answer, many questions concerning the authorship and origins of biblical texts. These questions are recognized as perfectly valid by evangelicals; the answers given by some critics have, however, sometimes been extremely embarrassing, not only to evangelicals, but to others of orthodox persuasion. The reason for this embarrassment is not difficult to discern: some of the critics' findings have often seemed to be irreconcilable with the view that the whole Bible is the inspired and trustworthy Word of God. Some critics have argued that the Bible is historically inaccurate, internally contradictory, and theologically mistaken. David Edwards speaks of 'innumerable passages' which are 'contradicted either by other passages in the Christian Bible or by the proofs or probabilities of modern historical knowledge'.[17]

Evangelicals have responded in various ways to this challenge. Some have concluded that the critical argument does indeed compel us to abandon the traditional Christian and evangelical view of Scripture, and that we must recognize Scripture as a fallible (though inspired) witness to divine revelation. Others have dismissed criticism as irresponsible and irrelevant, retreating into a dogmatic and simplistic fundamentalism. The one reaction represents the triumph of criticism over tradition, and the promotion of reason at the expense of revelation; the other represents a retreat from reason and from serious engagement with modern thought.

Many evangelicals, rightly in our view, have trodden a path between these two views, welcoming the critical method in principle, yet denying that its implementation necessarily undermines, in theory or practice, the historic Christian conviction concerning the divine authority of Scripture. Their response, then, to biblical criticism is both negative and positive.

Negatively, evangelicals have argued that all critics are influenced by their own cultural, philosophical and theological presuppositions, and that much of the criticism that has seemed to undermine the authority of Scripture has reflected a deep-rooted prejudice against the miraculous, which rests upon rationalist rather than Christian presuppositions. Even scholars whose work has been in other ways especially illuminating have sometimes found it hard to come to terms with biblical miracles and prophecy.[18] Evangelicals reject criticism based on such prejudice as, in the first place unchristian, and in the second as based upon a flawed methodology, in which a secular worldview is imposed upon the biblical material. Evangelicals have also pointed out that many critical conclusions are actually quite tentative and uncertain. Theories that were once regarded as 'assured results of criticism' – such as the JEDP theory of Pentateuchal origins, the 'Two Source' solution to the synoptic problem, or the controlling belief that Jesus' parables only make one simple point – are now seen to be at best questionable, and at worst definitely mistaken.[19] Biblical critics often appear to overlook the sheer provisionality of scholarship.

Both these tendencies are noted and criticized by New Testament scholar Walter Wink who points out how, in the past, scholars were notoriously dogmatic about what could *not* have happened in the New Testament:

> Historians still can demand that adequate warrants or evidence be produced for believing that something unusual has happened ... They can provide invaluable checks on superstition by casting a critical eye on extraordinary claims that have a tendentious bent. But to go beyond this to dogmatic assertions that faith healing, or clairvoyance, or resuscitation of the dead is impossible, is to go beyond one's competence as a historian to the faith assertions of a person caught in the narrow confines of a particular world view – or what Paul Ricoeur has called 'the available believable'.[20]

Too easily, the critics' approach to Scripture can become trapped within the rigid and narrow worldview of an ideology, which refuses to contemplate that anything beyond its own experience of the world could ever have taken place, or that any ideas alien to its outlook could be correct. At such points, criticism would seem to have overstepped its proper limits; Scripture is being judged on the basis of a transient and provisional understanding of reality, unaware of its own limitations and provisionality. The evangelical is no more free of presuppositions than the liberal, rationalist or secularist. Nevertheless, evangelicals insist that they are concerned to approach Scripture on its own terms, rather than imposing a modernizing straitjacket upon it, and that this approach leads to a sympathetic and intellectually satisfying reading of Scripture.

Yet evangelicals, while pointing out the limitations of biblical criticism, have also responded *positively* to some of its findings. The critical method is welcomed, because it takes seriously the incarnational principle, of which we spoke before; God has chosen to reveal himself not in some timeless ahistorical form, nor in abstract propositions, but in particular historical contexts and through real historical people. To understand God's self-revelation in history it is therefore necessary to understand those contexts and those people; the critical exploration of the human side of Scripture is a means to that end. Evangelical scholars have therefore embraced the method themselves, and contributed significantly to the critical enterprise.[21] The method has its limitations, as we have seen; indeed, some scholars have recently been quite negative about the potential of the historical approach to Scripture. However, although it is correct to recognize that all understanding of Scripture is partial and to some degree provisional, this cannot be interpreted to mean that the historical enterprise is dispensable or impossible. It is not dispensable, on account of the historical nature of Scripture itself; nor is it impossible, as has been shown by the fruitfulness of the method when applied – for example, an understanding of Ancient Near Eastern law and legal forms has illuminated enormously the meaning and distinctiveness of the Old Testament law codes; form criticism has contributed significantly to our appreciation of the Psalms; recent sociological approaches have opened up new ways of understanding both Old and New Testaments. Evangelicals have welcomed many of these insights.

In response to the findings of modern criticism, there is an increased recognition of the need to distinguish issues of hermeneutics and issues of authority. For example, is the authority of 2 Peter ultimately dependent upon Petrine authorship? Such issues are being given increasing attention within evangelicalism. A total commitment to biblical authority need not, some would argue, commit a scholar to a particular approach to biblical interpretation. An important and potentially difficult debate is emerging within an evangelicalism which no longer feels the need to be defensive over its commitment to either biblical scholarship or biblical authority.

Biblical authority and personal experience

A final element in any account of biblical authority is that of its subjective conviction – an idea expressed in quite different manners as 'the ring of truth' (J. B. Phillips) or 'the internal testimony of the Holy Spirit' (John Calvin). When the Bible is received and taught as the Word of God, it speaks to people's needs and situations with a power and relevance that confirm its inherent God-given authority. The gospels describe how Jesus electrified his audiences through his authoritative preaching; that authority was something that was in the first instance experienced, and only in the second explained, by his followers. The evangelical testimony is that Scripture comes to us as the self-authenticating and convincing Word of God. W. Robertson Smith expressed it thus:

> If I am asked why I receive Scripture as the Word of God . . . [I answer] . . . *Because the Bible is the only record of the redeeming love of God, because in the Bible alone I find God drawing near to us in Jesus Christ, and declaring to us in him his will for our salvation. And this record I know to be true by the witness of his Spirit in my heart, whereby I am assured that none other than God himself is able to speak such words to my soul.*[22]

Inevitably, this runs a risk of subjectivism. Yet, as Søren Kierkegaard reminded us, 'subjectivism' is not entirely a negative notion. In its deepest sense, 'subjectivism' means that something has inward relevance and applicability; in short, it has existential relevance. In his *Unscientific Postscript*, Kierkegaard stressed the need for 'an appropriation process of the most passionate inwardness'. Scripture, as we have seen, possesses a strongly objective dimension, in that it tells us about the way things are; it also possesses a subjective component, through which it offers to transform our inner lives – an offer which, in the evangelical experience, is more than justified, and leads to an emphasis upon evangelism as the means by which others might share in this same 'transforming friendship' (James Houston).[23]

Conclusion

'These are written that you may believe that Jesus is the Christ, the Son of God, and that by believing, you may have life in his name' (John 20.31). This verse may be seen as bringing together the converging evangelical emphases upon the authority of Scripture, the centrality of Jesus Christ, and the evangelistic imperative. Evangelicals accept the authority of the Bible, because they believe in Christ, and they follow through the implications of this belief, recognizing that Scripture and Christ are inseparable in practice. For to take *Scripture* seriously is, in the end, simply to take *Christ* seriously – which is the task and privilege of all authentically Christian theology, to which Anglicanism is a legitimate heir.

Notes

1. Karl Barth, *Church Dogmatics* 14 vols (Edinburgh: Clark, 1936–75), II/2, pp. 52–4.
2. Arthur Michael Ramsey, *God, Christ and the World* (London: SCM Press, 1969), p. 98. Similar views are, of course, expressed by Ramsey's mentor, William Temple.
3. See, among others, John Wenham, *Christ and the Bible* 2nd edn (Leicester: Inter-Varsity Press, 1984).
4. John Barton, *People of the Book?* (London: SPCK, 1988), p. 83.
5. *Ioannis Calvini opera quae supersunt omnia* 59 vols (Braunschweig/Berlin: Schwetschke, 1863–1900), vol. 9, p. 815, 'Mais fault que nostre entendement soit du tout arresté à ce poinct, d'apprendre en l'Escriture à cognoistre Iesus Christ seulement'.
6. See David Wenham, ed., *The Jesus Tradition outside the Gospels* (Sheffield: JSOT, 1984); more briefly, R. T. France, *The Evidence for Jesus* (London: Hodder & Stoughton, 1986), pp. 19–85.
7. Stephen Neill, *The Supremacy of Jesus* (London: Hodder & Stoughton, 1984), pp. 9–17. Perhaps his finest popular exploration of this theme is to be found in *The Challenge of Jesus Christ* (Madras: SPCK India, 1944).
8. *The Barmen Theological Declaration*; Arthur Cochrane, ed., *Reformed Confessions of the Sixteenth Century* (London: SCM Press, 1966), p. 334.
9. John Milbank, 'The End of Dialogue', in G. D'Costa, ed., *Christian Uniqueness Reconsidered: The Myth of a Pluralistic Theology of Religions* (Maryknoll, NY: Orbis, 1990), pp. 174–91; quote at p. 176. This essay merits detailed reading.
10. See George Lindbeck, *The Nature of Doctrine* (London: SPCK, 1984).
11. Alasdair MacIntyre, *Whose Justice? Which Rationality?* (Notre Dame, IN: University of Notre Dame, 1988), p. 6.
12. Raymond Aron, *Dimensions de la conscience historique* (Paris: Gallimard, 1961), p. 52.
13. See further: J. I. Packer, *'Fundamentalism' and the Word of God* (London: Inter-Varsity Press, 1958), pp. 80–1; 82–4; I. H. Marshall, *Biblical Inspiration* (London: Hodder & Stoughton, 1982), pp. 40–7.
14. Alan Richardson, *Preface to Bible Study* (London: SCM Press, 1943), p. 13. Michael Ramsey remarks, in commenting on Anglicanism during the period 1889–1939: 'There was for all typical Anglicans, not least those of the Anglo-Catholic school, no hesitancy on the cardinal doctrine . . . that Holy Scripture is the supreme authority in doctrine.' *From Gore to Temple* (London: Longmans, 1960), p. 166.
15. Barton, *People of the Book?*, p. 74.
16. Packer, *'Fundamentalism' and the Word of God*, p. 48.
17. David L. Edwards with John Stott, *Essentials: A Liberal–Evangelical Dialogue* (London: Hodder & Stoughton, 1988), p. 73. The discussion of evangelical beliefs in this book is especially illuminating.

18. William Barclay, writing at a popular level, was a respected scholar who rationalized the miracles. Gerd Theissen at least hints at such rationalization in *The Shadow of the Galilean* (London: SCM Press, 1987), p. 120. For evangelical scholarly discussion of such miracles, see David Wenham and Craig Blomberg, eds, *Gospel Perspectives 6: The Miracles of Jesus* (Sheffield: JSOT Press, 1986).
19. On the Two Source theory, see among others E. P. Sanders and M. Davies, *Studying the Synoptic Gospels* (London: SCM Press, 1989); on the parables, see C. L. Blomberg, *Interpreting the Parables* (Leicester: Inter-Varsity Press, 1990).
20. Walter Wink, *Transforming Bible Study* (Nashville TN: Abingdon, 1980), p. 155.
21. I. Howard Marshall is a case in point. His helpful study *Biblical Inspiration* is based upon lectures originally given at Wycliffe Hall. For some other discussions of inspiration from an evangelical viewpoint, see Packer, *'Fundamentalism' and the Word of God*. See also P. J. Achtemeier, *The Inspiration of Scripture* (Philadelphia: Westminster Press, 1980); W. J. Abraham, *The Divine Inspiration of Holy Scripture* (Oxford: Oxford University Press, 1981); K. R. Tremblath, *Evangelical Theories of Biblical Inspiration* (Oxford: Oxford University Press, 1987).
22. W. Robertson Smith, *Answer to the Form of Libel* (Edinburgh: Douglas, 1878), p. 21 (emphasis in original).
23. See Alister E. McGrath, *The Genesis of Doctrine* (Oxford: Blackwell, 1990), pp. 78–80. For a consideration of the relation of Scripture and doctrine, see pp. 52–66.

3

Evangelicalism and Biblical Scholarship

(1) The Old Testament

GORDON McCONVILLE

A new freedom

My task is to try to gauge the contribution of evangelical Old
Testament scholarship to contemporary evangelicalism, especially
within Anglicanism. When it is expressed thus it is clear that
certain attendant questions arise, and these should be mentioned
at the outset. First, modern evangelical scholarship in this country
is interdenominational, as are most self-consciously evangelical
movements. As an evangelical Anglican (by practice) with a good
deal of residual Presbyterianism, I want to identify with
evangelicals of other denominations, and I presume that my fellow
evangelical Anglicans do so as well. Nevertheless, Old Testament
scholarship is alive and well in Anglican evangelicalism, as I shall
indicate, and is part, I hope, of the vigour which currently
characterizes the phenomenon as a whole.

Second, the place of the Old Testament in the life and doctrine
of the Anglican churches is not so straightforward as that of the
New Testament. The perception of it as less authoritative and
relevant than the New Testament is reflected in the relative sparsity
of sermons and teaching based on it in the churches. By contrast,
in the world of scholarship the Old Testament has featured
prominently in debates about the nature of the Bible and its
authority. In an earlier generation in this country, biblical criticism
made headway first in Old Testament studies, perhaps because
some pious scholars believed that central issues of the faith were
less threatened there than in the New Testament. The Old

Testament has nothing quite comparable to Jesus' statements about his identity, or the narratives of his life and resurrection. Nevertheless there were always those who believed that the authority of the Old Testament was on a par with that of the New, and that this implied the need to defend its reliability. Indeed, in the early days of the Tyndale Fellowship (the society for evangelical biblical scholars), the lines seemed fairly clearly drawn between those who might be regarded as evangelical and those who might not, on the basis of whether they adhered to certain views about the authorship of Old Testament books.

A survey of the contemporary situation shows that matters have for some time stood otherwise. An issue of *Themelios* as long ago as 1977 featured a debate among three evangelical scholars (Gordon Wenham, John Goldingay and Robert Gurney) about the date of Daniel, with John Goldingay arguing that an acceptance of the later date did not necessarily compromise its authority, and indeed that it was better to read it as a second century BC document for exegetical and theological reasons.[1] (He has recently taken the same view in a substantial commentary on Daniel; Joyce Baldwin, in contrast, has argued otherwise.)[2] It is important to say that this is a kind of debate which can happen within evangelicalism. Members of the Tyndale Fellowship will in fact divide over many, perhaps all, of the issues which were once regarded as touchstones of orthodoxy. Evangelical theological colleges, too, embrace the same diversity.

This is not to say that the old 'conservative/liberal' debates are dead. It remains a real argument within evangelical Old Testament scholarship whether it is possible to stand within the critical mainstream without giving something crucial away. On one side of debates about the authorship of Daniel or Isaiah is an appeal to what the biblical books seem plainly to say or imply about themselves. On the other side is the argument that decisions about authorship are themselves dependent on exegesis and interpretation, which might lead to surprising results.

The debate is complex. Indeed, it may not be correct to call it a debate at all, for these days it rarely becomes one in any overt sense. As far as critical opinions are concerned, there is a freedom to explore and espouse a variety of views. Both in the wider evangelical world and in evangelical theological colleges, individual scholars and teachers are largely left to their own devices. And the result is that each will define for him or herself the boundaries which shall be acceptable. One will be conservative on Jeremiah but less so on Isaiah; another will be happy to read Jonah as a story without historical authenticity, but draw the line at reading the patriarchal narratives in the same way; another will plead that she does not know what to think about Leviticus because her teaching responsibilities have never obliged her to work it out.

This situation is neither a deplorable lapse from good evangelical standards nor mere anarchy. It reflects, rather, a definite shift in perspective. The argument has prevailed that responsible biblical interpretation cannot predetermine a set of acceptable critical opinions. James Barr's *Fundamentalism* may have been influential up to a point in causing evangelicals to look again at whether they were being as open to critical investigation as they thought they were. But it would be over-simple to see his work as the main reason for the change. It is rather, I believe, the complexity of the problem of the Old Testament itself, as a task for the church's interpretation, which has produced the present situation. The point is supported by a statement of J. I. Packer that a belief in the Bible's authority, even when that authority is framed as 'inerrancy', implies 'no advance commitment of any kind in the field of biblical interpretation'.[3] In a certain sense, the freedom of the individual scholar is an inevitable consequence of the historical character of God's revelation of himself.

Limits, and the need for relevance

Granted that a new sense of freedom exists in evangelical Old Testament studies, the question remains whether Christian scholars have unlimited freedom in the methods they adopt and the conclusions they reach in their studies. Such freedom can be presented as essential to any study which wishes to call itself scholarly; it may even be justified theologically by appeal to the idea of the Christian's freedom in Christ. New Testament studies, however, present an obvious problem to the idea of unlimited freedom in the shape of the resurrection narratives and their subsequent apostolic interpretation. Is there anything analogous in the Old Testament?

It seems to me that constraints are imposed upon evangelical Old Testament scholarship in two distinct ways, first by the need to avoid reductionism, and secondly by the need for relevance.

By reductionism, I mean those approaches to Old Testament study which suppose at the outset that the phenomena of the Old Testament can be adequately explained within the terms of one or more of the social sciences. An example is N. K. Gottwald's attempt to account for the rise and character of early Israel in terms of social realities: its mono-Yahwism and its non-monarchical tribal constitution were expressions of a kind of social revolution.[4] In a similar way, P. D. Hanson tried to describe the constitution of the post-restoration Jewish community in terms of a conflict between a central group that held power and a marginalized group, in terms that were borrowed expressly from Troeltsch and Weber.[5] As B. S. Childs has argued, such an approach to the Old Testament leaves little room for its own idea of God bringing into being an entirely new reality.[6]

Behind Childs's concern about sociological reductionism lie the fundamental questions of revelation, inspiration and authority. In what way can scholarship allow for these? Childs has crossed swords with Barr on this very issue. Barr argued that the Old Testament's own language about 'revelation' did not lead to the theological idea of revelation which had been adopted in much Christian thinking.[7] Childs replied that the idea of revelation was based on wider considerations than the terminology of 'revealing' and 'making known', and especially in the canonical idea itself.[8]

In trying to put limits on the freedom of the believing scholar, Childs has raised a banner to which a good many evangelicals have flocked. He himself cannot fairly be co-opted for the evangelical cause as such; indeed, he saw himself as providing a kind of bridge between conservative and liberal theology. Yet his work has seemed to some evangelicals to allow them to continue to hold to the ideas of revelation and biblical authority, and at the same time to explore and adopt certain critical views which not long ago would have been taboo. Childs's commentary on Exodus blazed a trail for an approach which gave free rein to the various branches of higher criticism, but accepted the whole text as finally authoritative on the grounds of its status as canonical.[9]

The influence of Childs on evangelicals may be seen, for example, in LaSor, Hubbard and Bush's *Old Testament Survey*. This volume, emanating from Fuller Theological Seminary, aimed to provide an introduction to the Old Testament for the evangelical student in the way that R. K. Harrison had done a generation earlier.[10] Like Harrison, LaSor et al. are concerned to defend the unity of the Pentateuch (to take an example). Whereas Harrison's idea of unity, however, was that the Pentateuch was actually Mosaic, LaSor speaks only of the 'prior importance of structural unity', and appeals expressly to Childs's canonical understanding of this.[11] J. Oswalt, in his recent commentary on Isaiah, seriously considers the Childs alternative, though he opts for the more conservative approach to Isaiah in the end.[12] John Goldingay too seems at times to come close to a 'canonical' interpretation, in his consideration of the diversity of the Old Testament Scriptures.[13]

Not all evangelicals, however, have been happy with Childs's answer to the problem posed by criticism. His concept of revelation located in the canonical process is an important shift away from the rather more 'prophetic' model of inspiration and revelation which has prevailed hitherto in evangelicalism.[14] Goldingay has also criticized his canonical method for undervaluing the dimensions of a text which he thinks historical study uncovers.[15] Childs's attractiveness to evangelicals is perhaps after all merely symptomatic of their need to think through again their understanding of the authority of the Bible in relation to the brass tacks of biblical interpretation and criticism.

Evangelicals are in fact doing this in their own ways. It is interesting to observe Goldingay reflecting on the relative claims of Jonah and the Books of Kings to be read as historical documents.[16] Gordon Wenham espouses an 'editorial' answer (rather than a strictly harmonizing one) to the old problem posed by the patriarchs' use of the name 'Yahweh' in apparent contradiction of the plain statement in Exod. 6.3; this, however, is in the context of an argument about the character of patriarchal religion, which both derives from and supports the Genesis picture of it.[17] The same author also wrote a persuasive defence of the unity of the flood narrative, that old chestnut of the documentary hypothesis, which is cited with approval in a recent (non-evangelical) re-appraisal of Pentateuchal criticism.[18] R. W. L. Moberly's treatment of Exod. 32–34 affirms the precedence of the theological shaping of the final form of the text over traditional literary critical analyses, while not denying the validity of these.[19] His attention to the final form leads him in fact to discover an editorial unity in the chapters, which he dates to an earlier period than is usually allowed. His work is not straightforwardly 'conservative', however, and despite his scepticism about the customary allocation of material to the sources J and E, he identifies the editor of Exod. 32–34 finally as the Yahwist, working in the tenth century BC.[20] The present writer has argued for an early date of Deuteronomy, and for Jeremiah's authorship of Jeremiah – in each case, however, in the context of an attempt to make a contribution to Old Testament theology.[21] It is in this context that I think critical issues should now be addressed; those issues, furthermore, must be treated individually on their own merits.

The modern debate about the Bible has shifted its ground in a way that I think is not entirely unhelpful. If there can be no return for evangelicals to a 'canon' of acceptable views about authorship, nevertheless, evangelical biblical scholarship derives a certain sense of direction from its understanding of the Bible as the Word of God. This, I think, is a better way of characterizing it than by seeing it as hedged in by certain 'no-go areas', even if a debate goes on within evangelicalism about what is permissible in terms of critical opinions. Furthermore, it is as evangelical Old Testament scholarship follows its vocation that it makes a real contribution to the wider discipline.

An evangelical contribution to Old Testament study

I said above that a second constraint imposed upon evangelical Old Testament scholarship is the need for relevance. This constraint comes from different quarters. One is the demand from a constituency which needs to see how study of the Old Testament affects the life of the ordinary Christian or the ordinary parish or church. Another is the pressure on the curriculum in the theological college, exacerbated by the shortness of the period of training for many ordinands. Yet another is the intrinsic difficulty of the Old Testament, whose inner relationships do not appear on the surface. This difficulty has been compounded in the eyes of many students by the development of Old Testament study into something of an esoteric art. The sigla 'JEDP' have become, in some quarters, almost a byword for obfuscation and irrelevance.

Most importantly, however, the pressure for relevance comes from evangelical theology itself. The belief that the Bible is the Word of God to the church in every age demands that it be made comprehensible, so that it might play its part in regulating belief and practice. The task for evangelical study of the Old Testament, therefore, is very close to that which has been identified by modern hermeneutics, namely to bridge the gap between the world of the Old Testament and the believing community of the present day (not that this is a new discovery for evangelicals!). It is this sense of mission which I think characterizes modern evangelical study of the Old Testament. It is not an easy task, for it cannot dispense with the historical dimension of the study (as some modern 'reader response' approaches freely do), yet it must understand the modern situation also, and indeed be governed by it in its choice of specific avenues to follow.

A couple of works by evangelical Anglicans may be mentioned because they understand and exemplify this task. Christopher Wright shows how the social and economic structures of ancient Israel are closely bound up with the theology and ethics of the Old Testament, and indeed establish patterns which are found also, in different forms, in the New Testament.[22] In doing so, interestingly, he draws on Gottwald's sociological analysis, which I have described above as uncongenial to evangelical concerns. Wright's treatment, however, avoids Gottwald's reductionism. His concern, indeed, for the relationship between Old and New Testaments, as well as the interest in ethics, is a good example of the attempt to marry genuine scholarly enquiry with relevance to the needs of the church.

In another important work, John Goldingay addresses the problem of Old Testament theology as such, trying in particular to deal constructively with what he sees as the theological diversity of the Old Testament literature. From an evangelical point of view the book can seem daring, when it asks such questions as, 'Can we affirm some (biblical) viewpoints and criticize others?' and undertakes an 'evaluative' study of the teaching of Deuteronomy.[23] Here, too, however, we find the same concern as in Wright, namely to appropriate the theology of the Old Testament and the experience of Israel for the life and faith of the church. An example of this in the book is its study of the idea of the 'people of God', the various manifestations of which are used to shed light on and evaluate understandings of the 'people of God' in the church today.[24]

Conclusions

There is a proper freedom for the individual Christian scholar. This belongs to the nature of the Old Testament as a set of historical documents, which must be investigated using valid historical tools. The central tenets of Christian faith, furthermore, do not *directly* require a particular view of any part of the Old Testament. In principle, therefore, evangelical Old Testament scholars may well find themselves in the mainstream of critical scholarship. However, I have suggested that they will indeed encounter limits to their freedom as they study the Old Testament in the context of Christian faith. The limits will be found in different places by different scholars. That is not necessarily bad, as long as there is constructive dialogue and mutual respect. There is no evangelical 'magisterium'.

For the evangelical scholar there is, however, a sense of vocation to the scholarly task. If the demands of scholarship and of faith seem to others to pull in opposite directions, there is perhaps no fully satisfactory response to this, except to proceed with the task in all integrity according to the lights one has been given. What matters is what one does with the scholarly tools which have been painstakingly acquired. And there, the primary responsibility, as I have said above, is to serve the church of Christ.

Notes

1. R. J. M. Gurney, J. E. Goldingay and G. J. Wenham, 'Approaching Daniel: Three Studies', *Themelios* 2 (1977), pp. 39–52.
2. J. E. Goldingay, *Daniel* (Dallas, TX: Word, 1989); J. G. Baldwin, *Daniel* (Leicester: Inter-Varsity Press, 1978).
3. J. I. Packer, *Under God's Word* (London: Marshall, Morgan & Scott, 1980), p. 53.
4. N. K. Gottwald, *The Tribes of Yahweh* (London: SCM Press, 1980).
5. P. D. Hanson, *The Dawn of Apocalyptic* (Philadelphia, PA: Fortress, 1975), pp. 211–20.
6. B. S. Childs, *Old Testament Theology in a Canonical Context* (Philadelphia, PA: Fortress, 1986), p. 25.
7. J. Barr, 'Revelation through History in the Old Testament and in Modern Theology', *Interpretation* 17 (1963), pp. 193–205; *Old and New in Interpretation* (London: SCM Press, 1966), pp. 65–102.
8. Childs, *Old Testament Theology*, pp. 20–3.
9. B. S. Childs, *Exodus* (London: SCM Press, 1974). The theory is stated more fully in his later *Introduction to the Old Testament as Scripture* (London: SCM Press, 1979).
10. W. S. LaSor, D. A. Hubbard and F. W. Bush, *Old Testament Survey* (Grand Rapids, MI: Eerdmans, 1982); cf. R. K. Harrison, *Introduction to the Old Testament* (London: Tyndale Press, 1969).
11. LaSor et al., *Old Testament Survey*, pp. 65f.
12. J. Oswalt, *The Book of Isaiah: Chapters 1–39* (Grand Rapids, MI: Eerdmans) p. 45.
13. See J. Goldingay, *Theological Diversity and the Authority of the Old Testament* (Grand Rapids, MI: Eerdmans, 1987), p. 189.
14. See I. H. Marshall's criticism of P. J. Achtemeier, whose position is close to that of Childs, in *Biblical Inspiration* (London: Hodder & Stoughton; Grand Rapids, MI: Eerdmans, 1982), pp. 37f.
15. J. Goldingay, *Approaches to Old Testament Interpretation* (Leicester: Inter-Varsity Press, 1990), pp. 130f.
16. J. Goldingay, '"That You May Know That Yahweh is God": A Study of the Relationship between Theology and Historical Truth in the Old Testament', *Tyndale Bulletin* 23 (1972), pp. 58–93.
17. G. J. Wenham, 'The Religion of the Patriarchs' in A. R. Millard and D. J. Wiseman, eds., *Essays on the Patriarchal Narratives* (Leicester: Inter-Varsity Press, 1980), pp. 157–88.
18. G. J. Wenham, 'The Coherence of the Flood-Narrative', *Vetus Testamentum* 28 (1978), pp. 336–48; cf. R. N. Whybray, *The Making of the Pentateuch* (Sheffield: JSOT, 1987), p. 83.
19. R. W. L. Moberly, *At the Mountain of God: Story and Theology in Exodus 32–34* (Sheffield: JSOT, 1983), p. 21.
20. Moberly, *At the Mountain of God*, pp. 185f.
21. J. G. McConville, *Law and Theology in Deuteronomy* (Sheffield: JSOT,

1984) and *Grace in the End: A Study of Deuteronomic Theology* (Grand Rapids, MI: Zondervan, 1992); *Judgment and Promise: Interpreting the Book of Jeremiah* (Leicester: Inter-Varsity Press, 1993).

22. C. J. H. Wright, *God's People in God's Land: Family, Land and Property in the Old Testament* (Exeter: Paternoster Press, 1990); see pp. 104–14 for a summary statement of the position outlined here.
23. Goldingay, *Theological Diversity*, pp. 97, 134f.
24. Goldingay, *Theological Diversity*, pp. 59ff.

4

Evangelicalism and Biblical Scholarship

(2) The New Testament

R. T. FRANCE

The idea of this volume arose out of an article which I was asked to write for the evangelical Anglican journal *Anvil* on 'James Barr and Evangelical Scholarship' (to which Professor Barr contributed a reply in the next issue).[1] The purpose of my article was primarily to evaluate the critique of conservative evangelical scholarship offered by Barr in his book *Fundamentalism* and in several subsequent works[2] and to assess how far his depiction of 'fundamentalism' corresponds to the way I, as an evangelical Anglican engaged in New Testament studies, and others like me approach our task. I believe that evangelical scholarship has much to gain from taking seriously some of the strictures made by Barr, particularly relating to biblical studies, and that the defensive and even dismissive stance which typically greeted Barr's 'attack' ('Well he would say that, wouldn't he?') was in danger of missing a valuable opportunity to see ourselves as others see us, and to learn from the experience.

As the article developed, I found myself led into more general reflections on the current situation in evangelical biblical studies, not necessarily related very directly to Barr's comments. This chapter, then, takes its cue from Barr's *Fundamentalism*, but ranges more widely. It takes up some of the issues raised in my *Anvil* article, to which reference may be made for fuller discussion.

Biblical scholarship is not, of course, a specifically Anglican concern. New Testament scholars do not, and should not, range themselves on denominational lines, and at a typical conference of

New Testament specialists there is little awareness of or even interest in the denominational affiliation of the participants. But I make no apology for the inclusion of this chapter in the book, since the current state of evangelical scholarship is a major factor in the self-understanding of evangelical Anglicans, and Anglicans have not been backward in contributing to whatever advances evangelical New Testament scholarship has made.

'Fundamentalism' and evangelical scholarship

I know few evangelical Anglicans who would call themselves, or would wish to be called, 'fundamentalists'. In the circles in which I move, the term is used predominantly as one of disapprobation, a designation for those with whom I do not wish to be associated. It might seem, then, that Barr's *Fundamentalism* is a strange place to start in considering evangelical Anglican scholarship.

However, many readers of the book, myself included, wrongly thought that Barr was simply equating 'fundamentalist' with 'conservative evangelical', if not even more generally with 'evangelical'. We therefore protested, as I did in my *Anvil* article, that it was unfair to saddle us with a name which we ourselves would repudiate, and thus by implication to condemn the whole evangelical scholarly enterprise by the unilateral imposition of a pejorative label.

Professor Barr's reply to my article makes it clear that this was not his intention. He has chosen his terms deliberately, and his target was not evangelical scholarship in general (indeed he uses the term 'evangelical' favourably, to denote the Christian tradition which he hopes to rescue from 'fundamentalism'), but those tendencies within it which are founded on 'inerrancy, infallibility and the other accompanying features' spelled out in his book, one of which is an innate hostility to modern critical study of the Bible, where it appears to lead in a direction incompatible with a doctrine of scriptural inerrancy. 'Conservative evangelicals' who do not exhibit this tendency (he singles out F. F. Bruce for honourable mention) are therefore not included in the book's strictures.

The question remains, however, how much of current evangelical biblical scholarship does in fact fall within Professor Barr's definition of 'fundamentalism', however much we might dislike the term – or at any rate how much residual 'fundamentalism' there is within the work of those of us who think of ourselves as evangelicals operating within the mainstream of critical scholarship rather than against it. Or, to put it the other way, how real is our commitment to critical study? Are we in fact willing to follow standard critical method only so far as our evangelical tradition, and the expectations of the evangelical constituency, will allow? Are we really playing the game by the accepted rules? Can we justly expect to be received as *bona fide* members of the scholarly guild?

At the end of his book Barr lists the 'conservative evangelical' (*sic*) works on which his research was based. The list contains many names very familiar to the present generation of evangelicals, including not a few Anglicans, such as Norman Anderson, Colin Brown, Michael Green, Derek Kidner, Leon Morris, James Packer, John Stott and John Wenham. Not all of these come in for equally strong censure, but it seems clear that the 'fundamentalist' writings with which Professor Barr takes issue are in many cases those on which the present generation of evangelical biblical scholars has been brought up. So, uncomfortable as we may be with his title, it is clear that the 'fundamentalist' scholarship on which Professor Barr focuses includes at least a part of what we would call (as he himself does from time to time) 'conservative evangelical'.

Evangelical New Testament scholarship – 1977 and beyond

The same year in which *Fundamentalism* appeared also saw the publication of a significant set of essays entitled *New Testament Interpretation*,[3] designed to show how evangelical study of the New Testament was relating to the methods and assumptions of mainstream critical scholarship. The essays displayed an openness to and an appreciation of contemporary critical currents which might have surprised earlier evangelical writers, and which some of the evangelical constituency of the time found disturbing. Yet the seventeen authors (eight of them Anglicans) are described in the editor's foreword as 'conservative evangelicals who combine a high regard for the authority of Holy Scripture with the belief that we are called to study it with the full use of our minds'. Here was, apparently, a 'conservative evangelicalism' which did not fit Barr's 'fundamentalist' image, or so its authors would have claimed.

Professor Barr's review of this collection is instructive.[4] On the one hand he disputes the term 'conservative evangelical': 'a good deal of the material could better be called liberal evangelical'; the position is 'a historical-critical one modified at points by residual fundamentalist elements . . . Here we have conservatives expounding methods which themselves are non-conservative and were developed by non-conservatives, often in the teeth of conservative opposition'; the book thus shows 'the slide of conservative scholarship towards a liberal position'. But on the other hand he chides the authors for their 'heavy historical (rather than theological) conservatism', and some of them for writing 'in a way calculated to confirm the most complete fundamentalist in his beliefs, comforting him constantly with assurances that Acts was written by a "first-class historian", that John is increasingly regarded as historically accurate, and so on'. His conclusion is that it is 'a book with two faces: it points in one direction and goes in another'. It might have been more consistent with the content of his review to say that it tries to go in both directions at once!

This review illustrates well the tension in which conservative scholarship must necessarily operate. There is in the mind both of evangelicals and non-evangelicals a clear image of what a 'consistently conservative' critical position must look like. It is an image which is defined to a large extent by contrast with mainstream criticism, both in its methods and in its results. The evangelical biblical critic who uses supposedly 'neutral' methods and/or who reaches conclusions which have not been traditional among evangelicals is therefore automatically suspect: fellow-evangelicals suspect him of 'liberal tendencies', while fellow-scholars suspect that he or she is merely pretending to use standard critical methods, while all the time the conservative conclusions are predetermined. Howard Marshall aptly compares the situation to walking along Striding Edge.[5]

As long as evangelical scholarship is perceived in terms similar to Barr's 'fundamentalism', there seems no possibility of a genuinely conservative evangelical engagement in New Testament scholarship outside the charmed circle of the 'fundamentalist' subculture. Yet increasingly since 1977 evangelicals have sought, and have gained, recognition as New Testament scholars, if we may judge from the number of people holding university New Testament teaching posts or publishing New Testament doctoral theses who are members of the Tyndale Fellowship or would otherwise identify themselves as evangelical.

Does this indicate then, as the logic of Barr's position would suggest, that they have ceased to be at least 'conservative' evangelicals (let alone 'fundamentalists', if any of them would ever have owned that title)? Some would, perhaps, be happy enough to shed the label 'conservative', as at best unnecessary and as liable to carry unhelpfully traditionalist (if not political!) connotations; but most would resist strenuously the suggestion that they have forfeited the right to be regarded as 'real' evangelicals.

What is 'evangelical' in New Testament scholarship?

I wish to sketch out here two examples, discussed also in my *Anvil* article, of the need, both on the part of evangelicals and others, to rethink what are the necessary implications of evangelical belief for New Testament study.

1. *Critical positions.* There is a long-standing tendency, both within and outside the evangelical constituency, to judge a person's credentials as an 'evangelical' by the positions he or she adopts on the composition, authorship and date of certain biblical books. Historically it is true that certain critical positions have been espoused, and doggedly defended, by evangelicals. But it is equally true that evangelical expectations in this area do not remain static.

There was a time when the Pauline authorship of Hebrews would have been regarded as part of evangelical orthodoxy, but that time has long gone. The apostolic authorship of Revelation is probably not now a majority evangelical position. Many evangelicals hold to the apostolic authorship of Matthew and John, but few would now regard this as a matter of evangelical faith. Even the Pauline authorship of the Pastorals, for long a touchstone of evangelical orthodoxy, is regarded by some evangelicals today as negotiable, while few would enter with enthusiasm on a defence of the Petrine authorship of 2 Peter.

But is this not simply 'the slide towards a liberal position' which

Professor Barr noted in 1977? Is not the integrity of a truly evangelical scholarship bound up with the reaffirmation of these traditional views? If evangelicalism were to be defined in terms of historical continuity, that might be so. But if it is essentially a theological position with its root in the supreme authority of Scripture as the Word of God, it should not allow itself to be bound by human traditions of literary criticism.

In the case of books like Hebrews, Matthew and John, which do not name their author in the text, or Revelation where the 'John' named cannot easily be identified, evangelicals can afford to sit loose to the traditional attributions, however much they may wish to support some of them on historical grounds. I have, for instance, argued that the apostolic authorship of Matthew seems to offer the most economical explanation of both the internal and external data,[6] but non-apostolic authorship would not cause me any theological problems. The fullest recent argument for the early date and apostolic authorship of John comes not from an evangelical but from a notoriously radical bishop![7]

But when the Pastorals claim to have been written by Paul, and 2 Peter by the Peter who witnessed the transfiguration, is not the veracity of Scripture at stake when their authorship is questioned? And surely that *is* a central theological concern of evangelicals, who cannot accommodate in their theology the notion that the formulation of the text is designed to mislead the reader at this point.

But that is precisely where discussion is, and must be, centred. Evangelicals who defend the pseudonymous origin of 2 Peter do so not on the assumption that a deliberate falsehood does not matter, but on the basis that a pseudonymous work deceived no one at the time when it was written, that it was an accepted and easily recognized literary genre, and that the equation pseudonymity = deceit is the result of reading back into antiquity the literary conventions of the modern world. In other words, the issue becomes one of *interpretation*, which brings me to my next point.

2. *The importance of hermeneutics.* The second National Evangelical Anglican Congress, held at Nottingham in 1977, in many ways confirmed and continued the directions adopted at Keele ten

years earlier. One issue which came newly into prominence, however, was that of 'hermeneutics', up to that point a word not much used outside the scholarly fraternity, but since then an accepted part of the normal evangelical Anglican vocabulary. It had always been recognized, of course, that Scripture needs to be interpreted, and that interpretations of the same passage will not always agree. But at Nottingham there was a new, and for many uncomfortable, realization of the complexity of hermeneutical issues, and of the cultural, historical and linguistic distance between the biblical world and our own, and also of the extent to which evangelical interpretation of the Bible had been governed by evangelical tradition rather than always by consciously approved hermeneutical principles.

But what was an unsettling new perspective for many ordinary church members has proved a liberating one for the evangelical scholarly enterprise. The issue of authorship mentioned above is only one of many ways in which the hermeneutical debate allowed traditional questions to be seen in a new light; what had hitherto been seen as simple issues of evangelical versus non-evangelical views came to be seen as areas on which evangelicals might legitimately differ. The result is, no doubt, that evangelicalism is a less outwardly coherent phenomenon than it used to appear, and that it is more difficult to define the shibboleths by which 'true evangelicals' may be identified. But that is a price worth paying for the greater freedom and creativity which has been brought into evangelical scholarship by the growing recognition that evangelical tradition may not always have said the last word on biblical interpretation.

One aspect of this development is that it becomes more and more difficult to characterize evangelicals as those who stand by the 'literal' meaning of Scripture. This was always at best a half-truth, since evangelicalism holds no brief for interpreting a text in defiance of its apparently intended meaning, and it did not take a debate on hermeneutics to reveal that much of the Bible is cast in figurative rather than literal language. Evangelical exegesis has always claimed to be looking for the 'natural' (or, in the more sophisticated term favoured by evangelical exegetes, the 'grammatico-historical') rather than the 'literal' meaning. The increasing hermeneutical awareness of recent years has merely made the traditional characterization of evangelicals as 'literalists' even more inappropriate.

The greater diversity in evangelical interpretation has, of course, created tensions within the constituency. Those for whom the evangelical tradition provides a secure point of reference are understandably anxious when evangelical New Testament scholars appear to want to remove the landmarks, by proclaiming 2 Peter pseudonymous, or by emphasizing the creative role of the evangelists at the expense of the harmonizing instinct which is deeply rooted in evangelical tradition. It is no doubt inevitable that those who are involved in the business of New Testament scholarship, and thus more aware of the problems raised by the text for a simplistic exegesis, will be perceived by many of their constituency as dangerously radical.

This area of discomfort is not new, and it is one with which we must be prepared to live if evangelical New Testament specialists are to continue not only to contribute significantly to their discipline, but also to bring some of the fruits of that discipline into the life and thinking of the evangelical churches. But it is to no one's benefit for this natural tension between the study and the pew to develop into mutual suspicion and hostility. An evangelical New Testament scholarship which is worth its name must listen as well as instruct, and must have as its primary aim to enable the people of God to live and think more responsibly on the basis of the Word of God, rather than to provoke or to discourage them by unnecessarily abrasive challenges to accepted interpretations.

Between 'fundamentalism' and 'liberalism'?

As was mentioned above, New Testament scholarship is not a denominational business. But I think that evangelical Anglicans may yet have a special role to play in relation to the issues we have been considering. At least their experience over the last quarter-century may offer an instructive paradigm.

When I was at theological college thirty years ago, most evangelical students had an essentially ghetto mentality. The wider world of Anglicanism was 'them' rather than 'us'. We were evangelicals first, and Anglican commitment came a poor second (and in some cases did not survive at all). Our attitude to mainstream biblical scholarship was similar: it was to be humoured for the sake of passing examinations, but little good was expected to come of it.

As far as our Anglican commitment was concerned, Keele (1967) marked a decisive shift from an attitude of suspicious adherence to one of committed involvement. Nottingham (1977) confirmed the same direction. Our commitment to biblical scholarship followed a similar course, though not marked by specific calendar dates; the publication of *New Testament Interpretation* was a sign of the times, and the hermeneutical discussions following NEAC2 were a natural sequel.

But not everyone in the evangelical Anglican constituency was happy with these trends. Dr Martyn Lloyd-Jones's appeal in 1966 to evangelical members of the main-line denominations to secede and join a 'pure' evangelical church met with little response among Anglicans, but some were almost persuaded, and became increasingly uneasy over the 'compromising' attitude of their fellow-evangelicals. There remains a substantial minority among evangelical Anglicans who share this unease.

The emergence of the journal *Anvil* in 1984 symbolizes the tension between these two tendencies. It results from a division between the editorial board of the long-established evangelical Anglican journal *Churchman* and its publishers, the Church Society. The catalyst was a New Testament study by Professor James Dunn (not himself an Anglican) delivered at the Anglican Evangelical Assembly in 1981 and published in *Churchman*.[8] Dunn's paper argued that the strictly 'inerrantist' view of Scripture taught by one influential strand of evangelicalism ('the Warfield position', corresponding quite closely to the 'fundamentalism' of Barr's critique) is contradicted by the New Testament itself, with its relatively free use of Old Testament texts. The publishers (representing what might be called the 'pre-Keele' strand of evangelical Anglicanism) objected to the editors including a paper which did not express 'a balanced evangelical position'. A parting of the ways followed, with *Anvil* coming into existence to express the more open stance of the former editors of *Churchman*.

It is from the *Anvil* perspective that this article is written. Here is, I believe, an appropriate middle way, an evangelicalism which is neither 'fundamentalist' nor 'liberal', and which may therefore be expected to contribute with increasing fruitfulness and acceptance not only to New Testament scholarship, but to the future character of the Anglican churches.

Notes

1. *Anvil* 8/1 (1991), pp. 51–64. Professor Barr's reply appeared in the next issue, 8/2, pp. 141–52.
2. James Barr, *Fundamentalism* (London: SCM Press, 1977). Significant subsequent studies include: 'The Problem of Fundamentalism Today', in Barr, *Explorations in Theology, 7* (London: SCM Press, 1980), pp. 65–90; *Escaping from Fundamentalism* (London: SCM Press, 1984); 'Fundamentalism and Biblical Authority', in A. Linzey and P. J. Wexler, eds, *Heaven and Earth* (Worthing: Churchman, 1986), pp. 23–37. The second edition of *Fundamentalism* (1981) contains a foreword responding to reactions to the first edition.
3. I. H. Marshall, ed., *New Testament Interpretation: Essays on Principles and Methods* (Exeter: Paternoster Press, 1977). The essays derived from the 1973 meeting of the New Testament Study Group of the Tyndale Fellowship for Biblical Research.
4. *Theology* 81, May 1978, pp. 233–5.
5. I. H. Marshall, *Biblical Inspiration* (London: Hodder & Stoughton, 1982), p. 7.
6. R. T. France, *Matthew: Evangelist and Teacher* (Exeter: Paternoster Press, 1989), chs 2 and 3.
7. J. A. T. Robinson, *The Priority of John* (London: SCM Press, 1985).
8. J. D. G. Dunn, 'The Authority of Scripture according to Scripture', *Churchman* 96 (1982), pp. 104–22, 201–25.

5

Evangelical Spirituality

GERALD HEGARTY

A work of art is like a crystal – like a crystal it must also possess a soul and the power to shine forth. It is not enough for a work of art to have ordered planes and lines. If a stone is tossed at a group of children, they hasten to scatter. A regrouping, an action, has been accomplished. This is composition.

Edvard Munch[1]

Too often Victorian images of evangelicalism have prevailed: many evangelicals rested content in the attenuated afterglow of mid-nineteenth century evangelical spirituality. It is now time for them to attempt a critical assessment of their own spirituality and its relation to other spiritual traditions. On the other hand, renewed interest in evangelical spirituality has led to diffuse productions; the impulse is frenetic, exploring writings and methods which seem to have little to do with evangelicalism. Somehow a shock has been administered to the evangelical spiritual tradition and the result is rather like the image Edvard Munch offers.

Munch's notes were written in 1929 at his final place of retreat, Ekely, near Oslo. His vision of the traditional elements of art being shattered, and by this action forming a totally new relation to each other, is an image of modernism. In the early years of the twentieth century this was the impetus of all that was new in art, exemplified by the work of Picasso, Schoenberg, and Joyce. The rupture with the classical forms was not a radical break, for the romantics had prepared the way and the modern movement could, perhaps, be seen as the logical conclusion of the romantic outlook, but in its final ironic mode. The ethos of modernism was radical and its method eclectic: disparate artistic traditions and cultures were

57

ransacked for the raw materials of the new art forms. It was urgent that a new construction was built before everything was lost under the impact of the modern situation. Despite the note of despair, the line from Eliot's *The Waste Land*, 'These fragments I have shored against my ruins', truly reflects the new view of composition.

This has also become true of evangelical spirituality. The avid piling up of spiritual fragments from the most diverse sources in an attempt to bolster spiritual life is becoming characteristic of many evangelicals' faith. It seems that the traditional way for evangelicals to draw together faith and life has been lost. Sometimes this loss has been taken to be a failure of evangelical spirituality, but it may be a failure actually to expound the evangelical way adequately. There is a need to see the genius of evangelical spirituality again, and this demands some understanding of its inner life, of its heart and mind, as well as the meaning of 'spirituality' itself. Evangelical spirituality also needs to be alert to its relation to the world as well as to God. If evangelical spirituality has come into a wider place it must again seek its horizon and recognize its boundaries as it finds renewed direction.

What is spirituality?

Although such a doughty champion of Calvinistic evangelicalism as Charles Haddon Spurgeon (1834–92) could use the term 'spirituality' to mean 'devotion' or 'piety', it is not a term which rests comfortably in the evangelical tradition.[2] The genesis and associations of 'spirituality' are inimical to the practical tradition of evangelical piety. For some understanding of the term 'spirituality' it is useful to turn to Owen Chadwick's clear summary of the word's mutation in meaning in its English and French use.[3] In England by the middle of the eighteenth century 'spirituality' had come to have, largely through the work of Roman Catholic writers, the meaning of 'devotion' or 'piety'. In France the term had secured its link with mystical or ascetic devotion by the late seventeenth century. It was thus a term of abuse, denoting the Quietist craving for the immaterial, the subjection of the body in the quest for the immediate presence of God. In both English and French usage spirituality emphasized the distinction between spirit and matter and signified a rejection of the material in the approach to God in prayer. Chadwick can quote Dr Johnson who, in 1755, included 'acts independent of the body; pure acts of the soul' among his definitions of 'spirituality'.[4]

The Roman Catholic usage has come to associate 'spirituality' with the 'inner life', or the 'interior life', thus making the connection with the mystical tradition. St Teresa of Avila's 'Interior Castle' is a model of this mystical piety, but even St Ignatius Loyola's *Spiritual Exercises* sustains and emphasizes the inner direction in non-mystical devotion. This tradition was foreign to English devotion in the modern period until the Tractarians introduced a renewed Roman Catholic spiritual practice, thus offering the young Anglican church a taste of one continental tradition.[5]

It is not difficult to see how this sits ill at ease with the evangelical emphasis upon practical devotion having a direct influence on character and 'good works'. Indeed, some evangelicals may feel uneasy with a tradtion which is orientated to indifference to the will and emotions and detachment from the material, whereas others may welcome such an invitation to a supposedly undeflected gaze upon God. Even in the Catholic tradition 'indifference' seemed to hold the danger of Quietism and the Holy Office of the Inquisition found it working to the neglect of public prayer and even use of the sacrament.[6] Thus, the term 'spirituality' has in its history and meaning a tension; pulling in opposing directions, the mystical and the practical jostle for their rightful place.

However, the alpha and omega of spirituality remains the vision of God, and so the presuppositions which suggest the direction, articulate the boundaries and form the framework for the creative struggle of spirituality are usually aesthetic. It is only from an examination of these presuppositions that evangelical spirituality can find its place in spirituality and an understanding of the fresh direction it seeks.

The aesthetics of evangelical spirituality

To be known, God is to be enjoyed. The calling and shaping of the self to make this possible is the intent of spirituality. What is to be employed in its pursuit is a matter of taste within the orbit of what is doctrinally acceptable. Aesthetics, the branch of philosophy which deals with the nature of art and the meaning of beauty, cannot be divorced from doctrine and spirituality in a Christianity where the eternal destiny of the Christian's life is to extol the beauty of the Lord. Evangelicalism cannot avoid aesthetic matters and has not done so, although its aesthetic tradition is not often considered. For example, in the first of his 'Jordan' poems George Herbert expounds an aesthetic which has passed into the spiritual life of evangelicalism:

> Who sayes that fictions onely and false hair
> Become a verse? Is there in truth no beautie?
> Is all good structure in a winding stair?
> May no lines passe, except they do their dutie
>   Not to a true, but painted chair?
>
> Is it no verse, except enchanted groves
> And sudden arbours shadow course-spunne lines?
> Must purling streams refresh a lovers loves?
> Must all be vail'd, while he that reades, divines,
>   Catching the sense at two removes?
>
> Shepherds are honest people; let them sing:
> Riddle who list, for me, and pull for Prime:
> I envie no mans nightingale or spring;
> Nor let them punish me with losse of rime,
>   Who plainly say, *My God, My King*.

Herbert's aesthetic is to identify truth with plainness, that which has a beauty of its own, needing no other adornment. Here is the Reformation's iconoclasm and desire for immediate understanding, the sense not caught 'at two removes'. The truth has a functional beauty – 'May no lines passe, except they do their dutie' – and the ornate only masquerades as fineness – 'sudden arbours shadow course-spunne lines'. This is very much a Reformation aesthetic. The Reformation iconoclasm of Zwingli and the Reformation whitewashing of church walls to obliterate medieval religious paintings, is the utter antithesis of the counter-Reformation Baroque accumulation of decoration and ornament in churches. The contrast appears again in the conflict between high church and evangelical; for example, in John Ruskin (1819–1900), the apostle of the 'Gothic' style and a deep influence upon tractarian church building, who claimed that, 'Ornament is the principal part of architecture'.[7] As an aesthetic this is uncharacteristic of evangelical taste, no matter how much some evangelicals may like gothic architecture. The evangelical tradition has taken Occam's Razor to unnecessary ornament and decoration, ritual is to be plain and unadorned, preaching to be direct. Evangelical spirituality has a functional aesthetic of 'form following function'. The essence of this aesthetic is well put by Oscar Wilde (1854–1900) in a lecture of 1882: 'All machinery may be beautiful, when it is undecorated even. Do not seek to decorate it. We cannot but think all good machinery is graceful, also, the line of the strength and the line of the beauty being one'.[8] Here is Herbert's vision restated, but also present is a premonition of the Bauhaus and the modern movement in design. It is a supreme functionalism where the beauty of the instrument succinctly attuned to its purpose is almost spiritual. Here is the parallel with evangelical spirituality where everything unnecessary to the goal of salvation and obedience to God must be jettisoned so that the disciple is ready for God, untrammelled by the cares of the world. God is to be found in the world, for nothing falls outside his grace. So, too, nothing is alienated from the scope of evangelical spirituality. Yet this functional aesthetic has been used to deny the virtue of art, something evangelicals are now finding both to reflect and enhance the worship and enjoyment of God.

This functional aesthetic sets the boundary for the consciousness of what counts as 'spiritual' for evangelicals. But because it relates to individuals it is a flexible boundary. The monastic movement, the ascetic life, the spirituality of the Baroque church, Bach chorales or Monteverdi vespers, any of these may be accepted by an evangelical on the ground that it is a means of drawing close to God, which for them has no excess but is perfectly fitted to their spiritual need. Yet, by itself, this aesthetic is only one part of what gives essential shape to evangelical spirituality, which stresses that the mind must be complemented with the heart.

The heart of evangelical spirituality

Christian spirituality is focused upon Christ. This is true for Catholic and evangelical, and aspects of both traditions intermingle when the cross is the subject. Catholic traditions of interest in the blood of Christ are close to evangelical responses to the same theme, so that Evelyn Underhill (1875–1941) can, for example, speak of the cost of discipleship as the only worthy response to the cross:

> [Worship's] full meaning is disclosed in the absolute oblation of the Cross. Cost is always essential to it. Thus wild animals and fruits are never used by agricultural people for the purposes of sacrifice. They must give something into which they have put their own life and work; for within that total, visible offering which is ritual sacrifice, is always implied the total invisible offering of the self, and everything the self best loves.[9]

Compare this with the themes of Isaac Watts's (1674–1748) hymn, a work close to the heart of evangelical spirituality:

> When I survey the wondrous cross
> On which the Prince of Glory died,
> My richest gain I count but loss,
> And pour contempt on all my pride.
>
> Forbid it, Lord, that I should boast,
> Save in the death of Christ, my God;
> All the vain things that charm me most,
> I sacrifice them to his blood.
>
> See! from his head, his hands, his feet,
> Sorrow and love flow mingled down;
> Did e'er such love and sorrow meet,
> Or thorns compose so rich a crown?
>
> Were the whole realm of nature mine,
> That were an offering far too small;
> Love so amazing, so divine,
> Demands my soul, my life, my all.

Here spirituality presents itself as glorying in the cross. The believer's life is bound up in the death of Christ, and all worldly accumulation falls away, the inner bastion of pride has become nothing. The pleasures and satisfactions of life are sacrificed in the sacrifice of Christ; the unburdening of the self leaves no ground for self-assertion, no basis upon which to boast. The work of the cross is successful: there is now freedom for a vision of God, to see the crucified one, his kingly crown veiled only in blood, that blood itself his love and pity for the world. The work of praise, which is the only and essential immediate response to God is finally seen to have a wider dimension: the whole of nature is insufficient to fulfil the offering of praise; the love of God demands the being and life of the worshipper. The hymn ends leaving the next step to be taken – to work out what self-offering in the world will be.

Here in a hymn at the very heart of evangelical spirituality is a powerful mystical sense. The theme of union with Christ leads to a vision of the crucified such that the demand of love absorbs all, soul and life, with the amazing divine being. This brings Watts close to the great Spanish mystic St John of the Cross (1542–91) for whom union with God is the overwhelming theme of the spiritual life. For John God can only be encountered when the persona of the self and its worldly trappings are inexorably stripped away:

> The lack of conformity with God's will can be had not only in one's acts, but in one's habits as well. Not only must actual voluntary imperfections cease, but habitual imperfections must be annihilated too.
>
> No creature, none of its actions and abilities, can reach or express God's nature. Consequently a man must strip himself of all creatures and of his actions and abilities (of his understanding, taste, and feeling) so that when everything unlike and unconformed to God is cast out, his soul may receive the likeness of God, since nothing contrary to the will of God will be left in him, and thus he will be transformed in God. (Ascent of Mt. Carmel II.5.4).[10]

In their understanding of union with God, Watts and St John of the Cross stand on the same ground. They are united in the sense of joy such deliverance from the world into the presence of God brings. Where they part company is in the level of explicit description of such a union. There is nothing comparable in Watts to John's poetry of consummation in the divine love. In his poem 'The Dark Night', John, moved by the Song of Songs, portrays the divine human as lover and beloved:

> Upon my flowering breast
> Which I kept wholly for Him alone,
> There He lay sleeping,
> And I caressing Him
> There in a breeze from the fanning cedars.
>
> When the breeze blew from the turret
> Parting His hair,
> He wounded my neck
> With his gentle hand,
> Suspending all my senses.
>
> I abandoned and forgot myself,
> Laying my face on my Beloved;
> All things ceased; I went out from myself,
> Leaving my cares
> Forgotten among the lilies.

And, in his 'Stanzas Concerning an Ecstasy Experienced in High Contemplation', he meditates on the knowledge found in union with God. It is so beyond what the mundane world conceives as knowledge as to be 'unknowing':

> This knowledge in unknowing
> Is so overwhelming
> That wise men disputing
> Can never overthrow it,
> For their knowledge does not reach
> To the understanding of not understanding,
> Transcending all knowledge.

Yet John knows that such a 'knowledge' is indeed a work of God:

> And this supreme knowledge
> Is so exalted
> That no power of man or learning
> Can grasp it;
> He who masters himself
> Will, with knowledge in unknowing,
> Always be transcending.

And here Watts would agree.

There have been those in the Puritan spiritual tradition who have also meditated upon the Song of Songs and have found the imagery of lover and beloved a metaphor of spiritual experience. They too have been led into the powerful, excited, sexual imagery which is evoked so strongly by St John of the Cross. But evangelicalism did not take this route, though Puritan tradition dabbled in it. This is not merely a reflection of the tension of 'indifference' with the practical work of faith, but a deep consequence of evangelicalism's deference to the limits imposed upon its spirituality by its aesthetic ground. Nor is it that John is not scriptural for he is a profoundly 'scriptural' writer, taking his themes from the Scriptures and appealing to many Old and New Testament texts in his works. It is that John has made more explicit what is barely hinted at in Scripture's description of the union with God. Evangelicalism has its mystical tradition, drawing on writers from Samuel Rutherford to Charles Spurgeon, who exhort believers to contemplate the beauty of Christ, something only those in union with Christ can actually do. Yet there is no claim in this that a special knowledge is vouchsafed, even if a particular realm of experience is thereby opened up. Evangelical spirituality desires to maintain a reticence about just this aspect of spiritual life. The union with Christ is something to be experienced, yet no one model of that experience is set forth. The only way it is to be described is in the terms set out in Scripture where the intimacies John portrays are absent. This is the constraint in evangelical spirituality, which directs the force of spiritual experience towards Christ, especially his work on the cross. The meaning of the cross is to be understood by a metaphorical expansion of the imagery present in the scriptural accounts. Here Watts succeeds wonderfully in allowing the physical reality of the crucifixion to be a hidden metaphor, undergirding the actual images used. In 'sorrow and love flow mingled down', the overwhelming image is of the blood of Christ, the touchstone of evangelical spirituality. But the word 'blood' is never mentioned: a triumph of the reticence inherent in the finest evangelical spirituality.

If Watts's hymn touches deep chords in the Catholic mystical tradition it also finds resonances in the practical transformation of the self envisaged by the Society of Jesus. Evangelical spirituality, as reflected in the hymn, bears comparison with the method of St Ignatius Loyola (1491/1495–1556) in his *Spiritual Exercises*.

The *Exercises* is a manual for personal examination of conscience leading into reflection and meditation upon the passion of Christ and so, ultimately, on to the transformation of the self. The attack on besetting sins, a change of will and a revision of behaviour is the dynamic of Ignatian practical spirituality, whereas meditation upon scenes of Christ's life and the evangelists' accounts recreated in the imagination is its inspiration. Finally the exercitant can attain a devotion to Christ and indifference to material things and worldly conditions which will leave him free to be a soldier of Christ. The elements of self-control and indifference find testimony in the full title of the work, which in English is, 'Spiritual exercises which have as their purpose the conquest of self and the regulation of one's life in such a way that no decision is made under the influence of any inordinate affection'.[11] The elements of the Ignatian retreat programme combine under careful direction so that they become the instruments by which the exercitant is moved to a deeper commitment to Christ, to be able to pray:

> Take Lord, and receive all my liberty, my memory, my understanding, and my entire will, all that I have and possess. Thou hast given all to me. To Thee, O Lord, I return it. All is Thine, dispose of it wholly according to Thy will. Give me Thy love and Thy grace, for this is sufficient for me.[12]

The influence of the 'Spiritual Exercises' in forming lives of practical devotion to the cause of Christ enabled many Jesuits to be faithful even to death. The long tradition of the spiritual efficacy of martyrdom reveals the power of the vision of Christ in providing the impetus for disciples to offer everything for the cause of Christ. If Foxe's *Book of Martyrs*, published in English in 1563, is a piece of Protestant propaganda, it is also testimony to the existence of the theme of martyrology within the Reformation tradition. It is given a refined spiritual shape by Watts, which echoes the Ignatian ideal that devotion to Christ demands the whole life given as an offering to the love of Christ. The point of difference with the Jesuit tradition is that Watts is portraying an encounter in worship which changes the self, whereas the means of change in the Ignatian tradition is through spiritual direction. The Exercises are a concentrated course, given by a spiritual director, with a definite goal ahead. Evangelical spiritual direction has never been concentrated in a course set out in a manual such as that provided by St Ignatius. The sermon, catechizing and spiritual counsel have been the methods evangelicals have used. Nevertheless in evangelical spirituality the aesthetic demand for clarity, plainness, attention to essentials, dislike of details superfluous to the work of knowing and obeying God, makes Ignatian spirituality an attractive resource. This is fostered by their kinship of goal which makes exploration of the Ignatian tradition appealing to evangelicals. Spiritual direction is a means, and the tradition of direction in the Exercises is not inimical to evangelicalism.

The heart of evangelical spirituality, then, urges the disciple on to the vision of God in mystical union. No matter in how restrained a fashion this may be described, a profound landscape of spiritual vision is opened by the recognition that this is part of the evangelical inheritance and may, perhaps, be claimed as the supreme focus of it. If this is indeed the climactic aspiration of evangelical spirituality then it is true that it enters into conflict with the aspirations of practical discipleship, of what it means to bear witness to Christ in the world, within history and culture.

The tension in evangelical spirituality

In his 'Types of Spirituality' in *The Study of Spirituality*[13] Geoffrey Wainwright has set out a theological framework for spirituality, based on the typology found in Richard Niebuhr's *Christ and Culture*. In Wainwright's reformulation there are two major, but extreme types. The first of these, 'Christ against culture', finds the world evil and hostile to the Christian faith; an inexorable gulf separates Christ from the world. The second position, 'the Christ of culture', affirms the world, but to the extent of leaving notions such as 'fall' and 'redemption' redundant.

Between these two extremes lie three mediating stances. 'Christ above culture' maintains that grace perfects nature, and human knowledge is subservient to the wisdom from above. The direction of worship is eschatological, glorying in the cross, in the Lamb who was slain. The second mediating position finds 'Christ and culture' in paradox. This lies on the world-negating side, emphasizing spiritual conflict in the world. Discipleship is focused upon prayer and the struggle with the world, the flesh and the devil. The present world is in opposition to the world of the kingdom. All human attempts at liturgy and sacrament stand condemned by their rational genesis. This journey leads to the borderland of the extreme charismatic, for whom the only authentic experience of God is found in ecstatic experience. It links with the world of the mystic for whom all worldly reality is subdued by contrast with the burning heart of the experience of the divine. The final mediating position is 'Christ the transformer of culture'. This rests on a positive doctrine of creation and incarnation, yet acknowledges the radical corruption of humanity. The believer is to be transformed into the likeness of Christ, just as the sacraments put forth symbolically the transformation from death to life in and through Christ. A 'transformation witness', such as that of the Jesuits, the Salvation Army and some evangelical missionary work, is to be the task of the church. An earthly kingdom is called to become the anticipation of the kingdom of God.

This is a useful framework. When applied to evangelicalism it reveals the tensions within evangelical spirituality, a spirituality which partakes of each of the mediating categories and so is finally caught in the polarization of the first two, world-denying and world-affirming.

The glorying in the cross which is central to evangelicalism can lead to withdrawal from the world, quietistically awaiting the eschaton. Yet this is traditionally modified in evangelicalism by the understanding of the world in conflict with the kingdom – the foolishness of God is wiser than the world, so fellowship with God and the church becomes the key Christian activity. Evangelism is primarily an invitation to come out of the world and into the church, and the conflicts Christians have in the world serve no worldly good, but only tend to draw one closer or lead one further away from God. In this model holiness of life can lead to experience of the mystical union with God. This is why Spurgeon is sometimes seen as an evangelical mystic.[14] His meditation on the believer's union with Christ led him to use language and imagery from the Song of Songs which place him close to St John of the Cross. It is at this point that the functional aesthetic of evangelicalism gives way to mystic rapture, so Spurgeon can say of Christ:

All loveliness meets in Him. He is the gathering up of all sorts of loveliness . . . His is an approachable beauty . . . He has within himself an unquenchable flame of love, which sets our soul on fire . . . Put together all loves . . . and they only make a drop compared with His great deeps of love, unexplored and unexplorable.[15]

Spurgeon was a Calvinistic Baptist, and indeed his way of understanding and extolling Christ is more characteristic of the Calvinist spirituality of Robert Murray McCheyne (1813–43) or Samuel Rutherford (1600–61). Nevertheless, Spurgeon is one of the great evangelicals, and in approaching the language and experience of mysticism in this way Spurgeon represents one of the lesser known sides of evangelical spirituality.

The last of the mediating themes of Christ transforming culture also exists in evangelical spirituality. Recently it has found a more radical voice, but a close look at the spiritual writings of many evangelical missionaries displays it too. As with the Jesuits, the transformation of culture is linked with the transformation of the self. Evangelical spirituality has not found this easy since the functional aesthetic has given a pre-eminence to salvation out of the world and into union with Christ. There is a strong tension between the desire to know God and the value of redeeming the world for God. Here too is a creative point for evangelical spirituality to pursue.

Composing evangelical spirituality

A new pattern of evangelical spirituality is emerging, yielding a challenge to those who think and give direction on spiritual matters. The functional aesthetic has limited and controlled evangelical spirituality, holding it back from mysticism and from profound commitment to the transformation of culture. This has enabled evangelicals to be critical of extreme pietism and fundamentalism. Yet if there is to be an evangelical spirituality which is theologically co-ordinated, the key task is to examine the aesthetic undergirding that spirituality. If the functional aesthetic is not to be denied, how can it now approach the questions which radical transformation and the mystical path present? Questions of spiritual direction, the use of spiritual resources from other traditions and the understanding of evangelicalism's own spirituality are founded upon the aesthetic question, and so the vitality and dynamic of evangelical spirituality can only receive theological direction from that source. But it is a spirituality irrevocably bound to the cross. No new direction in evangelical spirituality can avoid meditating on the meaning of the blood of Christ shed for the life of the world.

Notes

1. Quoted in Herschel B. Chipp et al., eds, *Theories of Modern Art* (Berkeley: University of California Press, 1968), p. 115.
2. C. H. Spurgeon, *Lectures to My Students* (London: Passmore and Alabaster, 1877), p. 57.
3. Owen Chadwick, 'Indifference and Morality', in Peter Brooks, ed., *Christian Spirituality: Essays in Honour of Gordon Rupp* (London: SCM Press, 1975).
4. Chadwick, 'Indifference and Morality', p. 205.
5. Chadwick, 'Indifference and Morality', p. 206.
6. Chadwick, 'Indifference and Morality', p. 216.
7. Nikolaus Pevsner, *Pioneers of Modern Design* (Harmondsworth: Penguin, 1974), p. 19.
8. Quoted in Pevsner, *Pioneers of Modern Design*, p. 27.
9. Quoted in Paul V. Marshall, 'Anglican Spirituality' in F. C. Senn, ed., *Protestant Spiritual Traditions* (New York: Paulist Press, 1986), p. 157.
10. In K. Kawanaugh OCD, ed., *The Collected Works of St John of the Cross* (Washington: Institute of Carmelite Studies, 1979).
11. Louis J. Puhl SJ, *The Spiritual Exercises of St Ignatius* (Chicago: Loyola University Press, 1951), p. 11.
12. Puhl, *The Spiritual Exercises of St Ignatius*, p. 102.
13. Geoffrey Wainwright, 'Types of Spirituality', in Cheslyn Jones et al., eds, *The Study of Spirituality* (London: SPCK, 1986), pp. 592–605.
14. W. James Gordon, *Evangelical Spirituality: From the Wesleys to John Stott* (London: SPCK, 1991), pp. 161f.
15. Quoted in Gordon, *Evangelical Spirituality*, p. 162.

6

Evangelicalism and the Sacraments

PETER SOUTHWELL

Two of the most valuable contributions of the evangelical movement to the spiritual life of the Anglican churches are its commitment to the primacy of Scripture in theological thinking and its emphasis on personal conversion to Christ. It is in part because some of the churches' sacramental practices apparently find no support in Scripture, or are even implicitly condemned in its pages, that evangelical Anglicans have traditionally underplayed the place of sacramental worship in our corporate life. Thus, to give one example, our Lord's frequently reported strictures upon those who like to wear long robes, enjoy the chief seats in places of worship, accept titles and public acclaim, or who like to make a display of their piety, present some serious challenges to the way our present bishops and other clergy conduct their public ministry in today's church, whether willingly or not. When this is taken in conjunction with the condemnation by some Old Testament prophets of ancient Israel's sacrilegious tendency to prize the means of grace above the giver of grace, then it can readily be seen how a Christian who knows those parts of the Bible may well feel ill at ease in a church which ostensibly falls into such traps in its own sacramental worship. This the Anglican churches undoubtedly do.

The emphasis evangelicalism places on personal conversion to Christ has also been a cause of its adherents' aversion to placing the Holy Communion at the centre of their Sunday worship. One influential evangelical leader has even been known to recommend keeping the Holy Communion at 8.00 a.m. 'for keen people', so as to make Morning Prayer available (and adaptable) for 'fringe' members of the church, or for outsiders. This of course cuts right across the tendency of the liturgical movement to restore the eucharist to its primacy in corporate and public worship. The decision of the National Evangelical Anglican Congress at Keele University in 1967 to 'work towards the practice of a weekly celebration of the sacrament as the central corporate service of the church'[1] was not taken without opposition, and is even now honoured nearly as much in the breach as in the observance. Part at least of the motivation of such reluctance to honour our Lord thus in the *sacrament* of his death is the desire to honour him in the evangelistic *proclamation* of his death in less 'churchy', more informal, family- and outsider-orientated worship. The older allegiance to Morning Prayer is, however, fast fading, its residual elements diminishing quietly like the smile of the Cheshire cat.

A third element in this apparent devaluation of the Holy Communion would in fact be regarded by many evangelicals as a revaluation of it, namely the desire to make it more special by less frequent attendance or even less frequent celebration. A nineteenth-century style of pietism (with strong non-conformist roots) is reinforced by reference to the Prayer Book direction that 'every Parishioner shall communicate at least three times in the year, of which Easter to be one' (*sic*) as good reason not to let familiarity breed contempt of a sacrament so holy. This attitude receives some endorsement in the Prayer Book's exhortation to 'all persons diligently to try and examine themselves, before they presume to eat of that Bread, and drink of that Cup . . . lest we kindle God's wrath against us (and) provoke him to plague us with divers diseases and sundry kinds of death'. As St Paul put it, 'If we judged ourselves [at the Lord's Supper] we would not come under judgement' (1 Cor. 11.31). There is in all this a godliness which current Anglican practices can dilute. St Augustine of Hippo saw in our Lord's warning against casting pearls before swine a reference to such abuse of the sacraments.

A fourth element in Anglican evangelical anti-sacramentalism is the fear of superstition. There can be no doubt that the Christian faith (like other religions, not excluding Judaism, Buddhism and Islam) has, over the centuries, acquired an admixture of superstitious belief and practice which constitutes a significant legacy of older religions. In addition doctrines have crept into Christianity, in connection with the Holy Communion as well as elsewhere, which have no foundation in the teaching of its founder. Thus an English missal, published as recently as 1957, can promise in a footnote (citing Pius X in 1906) that anyone who, adoring the Host at its elevation, says in his heart, 'My Lord and my God', will thereby earn seven years' indulgence, and a weekly plenary indulgence is offered to those who render such devotion daily. Of such attitudes to sacraments Bible-centred evangelicals are understandably chary. Evangelicalism is more cerebral in its liturgical ethos (witness its particular appeal to the middle and upper classes) than other traditions which (like the Old Testament) make use of symbolic images, and it is sensitive to the dangers of idolatry (though it can hold tenaciously to doctrines which are not scriptural, such as justification by faith only, or the authority and inspiration of Scripture only 'as originally given'). Devotion to a sacrament however is discouraged, sometimes even by quite cavalier practices in the treatment of the bread and wine which speak of Christ's body and blood. 'Do this in remembrance of me' maybe, but not with too much care or ceremony.

We come lastly, in this brief summary of modern evangelical attitudes, to the much-loved doctrine of the priesthood of all believers. A consequence of the belief that all Christians have equal access to God is that there can be no place for a class of ministers claiming a greater right than others to handle and administer holy things. That the priesthood of all God's people is an Old Testament doctrine in origin, and that nonetheless such ministers were ordained in Israel (the priests and Levites) is not often considered in this context, any more than the fact that the essential role of an Israelite priest was to teach. Evangelicals usually speak as though the essence of Old Testament priesthood was mediation between God and men. Once again, however, devotion to the old formula necessarily results in caution about any sacrament whose administration lies in the hands of what is perceived as a hierarchy within the church.

There is always the danger that strongly held convictions inhibit serious thought, and an equal danger that conventional practices become confused with theological principles. It is by no means the case that Anglican evangelical attitudes to the sacraments have not been the subject of recent theological publishing, from J. I. Packer's useful collection of papers read at the Oxford Conference of Evangelical Churchmen in 1961,[2] to the forthcoming *Evangelical Eucharistic Thought in the Church of England* by Christopher Cocksworth.[3] We shall shortly welcome Peter Toon's *Knowing God Through the Liturgy*.[4] It may however be useful at this point to indicate how evangelicals might think about the sacraments, the Holy Communion in particular, but not excluding baptism and indeed the non-dominical sacraments (that is, those described in Article XXV as 'commonly called Sacraments . . . not to be counted for Sacraments of the Gospel').[5] It must be therefore to the Bible that we first turn.

That worship of God should be offered with due reverence for its divine recipient is a clear concern of the biblical writers. The word 'worship' both in Hebrew and in Greek implies physical prostration, such as is still offered by Muslims in mosques (the word mosque itself means 'place of prostration'). The familiar words of Psalm 95 (the 'Venite' of Anglican prayer books) remind us, when we sing aloud to God, to recall his greatness and supremacy over all things; to kneel in worship; and to hear and heed his words lest we incur his displeasure. God is to be worshipped 'in the beauty of holiness' and the whole earth is to tremble before him (Ps. 99.6). The God-ordained rituals of Hebrew liturgy reveal his concern for the detail of public worship. We learn too, from the prophets especially, that worship should be offered from the heart as well as the lips (Isaiah 29.13), which our Lord himself echoes in his words to the Samaritan woman: 'Those who worship [God] must worship in spirit and in truth' (John 4.24). The Old Testament's revelation of God's concern for order is echoed also in the New, for example by St Paul ('Let all things be done decently and in order', 1 Cor. 14.40), and in the glimpses we have in the book of Revelation of the structured adoration of God and of the Lamb by saints and angels in heaven.

Thus it will be important for Christians, to whom has been entrusted the administration of sacramental water, bread and wine, as well as of anointing with oil and the laying on of hands, to pay due heed to these God-given principles of worship, both ritual and interior. Only the best can be good enough for God, so long as we have the resources to offer it, and thus the words we bring, the music we play, the quality of our prayers, reading, preaching and teaching, as well as of our meeting places themselves should express what we believe about God's beauty and holiness, as well as his closeness to our human condition.

In the New Testament itself we are taught four things about the sacrament of Christ's body and blood. In the first place we know he commanded his followers to 'do this in remembrance of me'. He took bread, gave God thanks for it, broke it and gave it to them with the words, 'This is my body given for you'. So too with the cup: 'Drink from it, all of you. This is my blood of the (new) covenant which is poured out for many for the forgiveness of sins' (Matt. 26.26–8 etc.). As therefore we obey his command and make this commemoration of his death for us we should do so with reverence, gratitude, solemnity and joy and savour each element in the re-enacted drama which links us in an unbroken chain down the centuries to the events in that 'upper room' so long ago, making them real afresh to our hearts and minds.

In some churches today our taking of the sacramental bread can seem cavalier and lacking gratitude; our offering of thanks can be perfunctory and superficial; our breaking the bread purely functional and far from being a dramatic picture of Christ's body being broken on the cross; and our distribution merely routine and unthinking. What he told us to do we should do well, as we remember his loving self-oblation for us.

In second place in this service we anticipate his glorious return to feast with us in heaven. 'Henceforth', he said, 'I shall not drink again of the fruit of the vine until that day when I drink it anew in the kingdom of God' (Mark 14.25). St Paul too remarks that in this act 'you proclaim the Lord's death until he comes' (1 Cor. 11.26). As we recall his sacrificial death for us we also celebrate in anticipation the 'messianic banquet' he promised to his followers (e.g. Luke 12.37). Such an occasion deserves to be conducted with every mark of Christian joy, thankfulness and love as, mindful of Christ's absence from us now, we eagerly await his glorious coming.

Third, in the Lord's supper we enjoy fellowship with one another: 'We, who are many, are one body, for we all partake of the one loaf' (1 Cor. 10.17). It is deemed proper to exclude from such fellowship those whom the Prayer Book calls 'notorious evil livers', and the same rite invites attendance by those 'who are in love and charity with their neighbours, intending to lead a new life, following the commandments of God and walking from henceforth in his holy ways' (see 1 Cor. 11.27–33). The reason is that it is a feature of the way Christians treat one another that we do all we can to maximize the degree to which Christ himself is present in each and all of us to minister to others. The service of Holy Communion is now, as it was in that 'upper room', a trysting place for us to meet with one another and with the Lord, and in so doing to enrich our experience of that fellowship by every possible means.

Lastly, and wonderfully, we are told that the Lord himself is present and that we feed, as it were, on him. Not only does the risen Christ invite his penitent disciples to sup with him (Rev. 3.20), but St Paul asks, 'Is not the cup of thanksgiving for which we give thanks a participation in the blood of Christ? And is not the bread that we break a participation in the body of Christ?' (1 Cor. 10.16), echoing the words of our Lord in St John's gospel (6.53–8), 'Unless you can eat the flesh of the Son of man and drink his blood, you have no life in you. Whoever eats my flesh and drinks my blood has eternal life, and I will raise him up at the last day.' We recognize here again the eschatological dimension we noted earlier, but the experience of eating and drinking is a present experience, and the word John uses for 'eat' literally means 'chew' or 'munch', thus creating a context of the very deepest intimacy. In this sacrament the Lord is not only absent (as we noted above), but intimately present to the believer. Such an occasion should not be marked by anything less than the greatest love, care and devotion in our liturgical practices.

There is thus, in what the New Testament writers have to say about the Lord's supper, no warrant for modern Christians neglecting to observe the rite, or for observing it carelessly, infrequently or reluctantly. Any danger of superstitious abuse of the sacrament or of false doctrine is avoided not by denigrating its place in our corporate life, but by enhancing it in ways which tell clearly and dramatically the story the rite itself has to tell, and this, together with faithful and true preaching and teaching, will result in congregations being exposed more fully to Christ in this means of his grace, and thus more effective in his service.

What is true of the sacrament of his body and blood is true also of baptism, anointing, the laying on of hands in confirmation or ordination and indeed all Christian sacramental rites, including marriage. Such rites have functions which are pastoral (i.e. they build up and enrich the spiritual life of those to whom they are administered, in their relations with God: they are, as it were, his touch of love and empowerment); theological (i.e. they tell, by sign and by word, things about God which are true and saving in their effects, so that we grow thereby in the clarity of our knowledge of God, and in the 'assurance of his favour and goodness towards us' (so the Book of Common Prayer); and also evangelistic i.e. non-believers who witness such rites may perceive in what is said and done the cogency of God's address to mankind in Christ, and may even respond to that address; see 1 Cor. 14.24, on the exercise of prophetic gifts in church). If, however, these pastoral, theological and evangelistic functions are to be effective, our practices in administering these sacraments should be such as to maximize and clarify what is signified by the sacrament in question. It is to how this is best done that we shall now, and in conclusion, turn.

One priority on the agenda of evangelical as well as other churches needs to be a resolution of the problem of how to meet the needs of children when they are in church with adults. To educate them separately in Sunday school classes has been a traditional solution to this need for teaching at the appropriate level and for more youth-orientated forms of worship. Another solution has been the 'family service', in which both preaching and liturgy are reduced to a level which may engage the minds and hearts of the young but does not necessarily meet the different needs of the adults present. It is in this context too that the question of children receiving the sacrament of the Holy Communion arises, with or without prior administration of confirmation. Practice varies nowadays amongst all the churches. The situation might be resolved by moves in the direction of making the Holy Communion central to most forms of public worship on Sundays, and admitting the young to it after due and careful instruction, but also providing (if space permits) differing modes of preparation and approach to that service for different age groups. Thus families would be together for the eucharist itself, with the exception perhaps of the very young. What happens in practice will of course vary from church to church, but the issue needs to be faced more squarely.

A weekly central communion service for families must necessarily involve as much lay participation as is possible, and clearly the quality of any offering of worship, sacramental or otherwise, will be enhanced by the use of as many appropriate talents as can be found amongst the congregation. It should not be assumed that the clergy are without peer in their liturgical gifts. Wide participation in contributing to worship should not however preclude careful rehearsal and training.

There is little point in inviting people to read if they lack reading skills, and the same goes for music, dance, drama and intercession, as well as preaching. Some have great gifts in these areas: others less so. Those tasks confined by law and tradition to the clergy (especially presidency at the eucharist) as well as those not so confined but encouraged in the New Testament (e.g. preaching and reading the Scriptures in public, 1 Tim. 4.13) are those for which they have been publicly commissioned at their ordination and for which also they have been trained. Presidency at the eucharist is especially appropriate to one who is called to govern a congregation (for the word see 1 Tim. 5.17), who also has the task we referred to above of exercising some discipline over attendance at that sacrament and ensuring that heedless reception does not lead to spiritual atrophy. It is where we are admitted to communion at the Lord's table by duly authorized ministers that we are in some ways most evidently the body of Christ. The increasing practice of lay presidency may be in danger of weakening the discipline Scripture requires in the church's public life.

What vesture is worn by officers of the church, especially in sacramental worship, has varied enormously down the centuries and across diverse cultures. It may seem to some ridiculous to expect clergy to wear a stylized version of medieval academic dress in the late twentieth century, or relics of Byzantine court dress or old Roman liturgical vesture. They are probably right – although all societies know instinctively that there is a place for garments of celebration, identification and historic association on certain great occasions and in certain significant places – and overmuch devotion to dressing up is one of the more ludicrous and self-regarding characteristics of office-bearers in all societies, the church not excluded. All that needs to be affirmed here is that whatever is worn by those who preside over our sacramental worship should be appropriate to those who are the ministers of Christ and the servants of his people, being duly mindful of whom they represent and in whose name they exercise their ministry.

Another way of ensuring that our awareness of God's grace to us in Christ is sharpened in the context of sacramental worship is a proper use of silence. There is a time for silence before there is a time to speak (Eccles. 3.7), and more than one prophet urges his readers to keep silence, because the Lord is in his holy temple (Hab. 2.20; compare Zech. 2.13). Silence is kept in heaven at the moment when the triumphant Lamb is about to open the seventh seal (Rev. 8.1), which is a strong pointer to its appropriateness when the climax of his earthly ministry is commemorated in the eucharist. The hymn from the liturgy of St James puts it well:

Let all mortal flesh keep silence,
And in fear and trembling stand;
Ponder nothing earthly-minded,
For with blessing in his hand,
Christ our God to earth descendeth,
Our full homage to demand.

It is good that in the Alternative Service Book as well as in other modern liturgical publications the use of silence is encouraged at key moments of a service, as for example after hearing a reading or sermon, during intercession or before receiving the sacrament. At these and other points decent periods of silence can sometimes enable the worshipper to savour what is happening more fully than when a service proceeds with a relentless and verbose progression towards some notional deadline. What should be avoided is the kind of service in which all the time available is given to extended and self-indulgent singing, preaching or intercession out of all proportion to other elements in our offering of worship to God: far better to save time from such things to use in silent contemplation of God in his beauty, stimulated chiefly though not only by word and sacrament, so as the more readily to digest the spiritual food we are being served by our Lord through his various ministers. 'Guard your steps' we are told 'when you go to the house of God. . . . Do not be quick with your mouth . . . to utter anything before God. God is in heaven and you are on earth, so let your words be few' (Eccles. 5.1-2). This applies as much to time in church before a service as to the conduct of the service itself. Even children can learn to love reverence and stillness.

These few paragraphs have thus constituted a plea for evangelical attitudes to the sacraments to conform more closely to those two distinctive marks of evangelicalism with which we began, that is, adherence to Scripture and concern for evangelism. We have found in the Scriptures good reason to be enthusiastic in our enjoyment of God's sacramental means of grace, and in particular to make the re-enactment of the Last Supper central to our commemoration of Christ's atoning death. While it is right that we should take pains to avoid ecclesiastical pomposity, over-familiarity with holy things, superstition and 'priestcraft', we have seen how scriptural principles and injunctions point us to ways in which we can and should enhance our sometimes rather reluctant, marginal and insecure sacramental practices in ways which make them more honouring to God and the greatness of his name. Further, to do this is also to maximize the evangelistic potential of the rites in question, especially the Holy Communion. The proclamation of the Lord's death for our salvation inherent in that rite serves well the varied pastoral, theological and evangelistic needs of those who witness or participate in it. Physical things matter: Christ's incarnation proves it. The ways in which God has invited us to use some of these – water, bread, wine and oil amongst them – are to our own souls' health as we meet him and he meets us, when we use them according to his command, according to scriptural principles, and with all the love, imagination and care to which the church's Spirit-taught mind can rise.

Notes

1. *Keele 1967: Report of the National Evangelical Anglican Congress* (London: CPAS, 1967), p. 35.
2. J. I. Packer, ed., *Eucharistic Sacrifice* (London: CBRP, 1962).
3. Christopher J. Cocksworth, *Evangelical Eucharistic Thought in the Church of England* (Cambridge: Cambridge University Press, 1993).

4. Peter Toon, *Knowing God Through the Liturgy* (London: Prayer Book Society, 1992).
5. See, for example, Martin Dudley and Geoffrey Rowell, eds, *Oil of Gladness* (London: SPCK, 1993).

7

Evangelicalism and Evangelism

GRAHAM TOMLIN

On 16 August 1739 John Wesley was summoned by Joseph Butler, famous for his *Analogy of Religion* published three years before, who was at the time Bishop of Bristol. The discussion did not go well. 'Well sir, since you ask my advice', concluded Butler, 'I will give it to you very freely. You are not commissioned to preach in this diocese. Therefore I advise you to go hence.' Thus one of the greatest Anglican philosophers banished perhaps the greatest Anglican evangelist. This incident highlights two crucial aspects of the relationship between Anglicanism and evangelism. One of Anglicanism's greatest strengths has been its reflective and careful intellectual tradition. This philosophical inclination has often been ill at ease with the enthusiasm of the natural evangelist. The result is that the Anglican churches have had an uncertain relationship with evangelism, never quite sure whether it is properly 'Anglican' or not. The second is that, consequently, evangelism has often been pushed on to the edge of, if not altogether outside, Anglican church life. Whether and how these two factors are resolved will determine to a large extent what happens in and through the Decade of Evangelism in the Church of England.

The Church of England and evangelism

The official Anglican approach to the issue in this century has largely taken the form of a series of forays into evangelistic territory when the church was reminded of its responsibility to the whole of the English people. The 'National Mission of Repentance and Hope' under Randall Davidson in 1916, followed by the Archbishops' 'Committee of Enquiry into the Evangelistic Work of

82

the Church' in 1917, the report, 'Towards the Conversion of England' in 1945 chaired by Bishop Chavasse, and Archbishop Coggan's 'Call to the Nation' in 1975, have represented the Church of England's evangelistic conscience at work. The one thing these impulses have in common, however, is that none of them appear with hindsight to have met with much success. What hope is there that the 'Decade of Evangelism' will meet with any more? Moreover, evangelicals have always seemed to be keen on evangelism, and they have tended quietly (or noisily) to get on with the job, while others in the church often keep their distance. Are there things which evangelical Anglicans have to learn from the reserve of others, and things which Anglican evangelicalism has to offer to the rest of the Church of England in creating a culturally relevant and genuinely Christian form of address to the nation of which it is a part?

One difference between the Decade of Evangelism and previous similar 'calls' lies in a shift of cultural and theological climate. These earlier efforts in evangelism give the impression of a church feeling it ought to be concerned for evangelism, yet not quite sure how to go about it. As the year 2000 approaches however, the increasing sense of the world as a global village and the rise in recognition of Britain as a multi-cultural society have forced the issue of Christianity's relationship to other faiths firmly on to the church's agenda. Ironically, since the call for a Decade of Evangelism, Muslims and Jews for example, are even more sensitive to being unfairly targeted by Christians for aggressive proselytization. This heightened awareness in fact makes evangelism a much more controversial, sensitive and disreputable activity in the 1990s than it has been before. Suddenly many in the church are not so sure whether we ought to be involved in evangelism at all.

This issue is of course the thin end of the pluralist wedge. It is a short step from arguing that, 'there is no question of converting, now or ever, to a "truer" view; for all traditions offer valid ways of relating salvifically to the one Ultimate Reality',[1] to questioning the validity of any attempt to persuade anyone in a pluralist society to change their minds. Evangelism of other faiths is seen as illegitimate, partly because Christians cannot claim to possess either the ultimate truth about God or the world, nor the key to the meaning of human life and history, and partly because such a claim is divisive and violates the paramount necessity of mutual tolerance for the sake of human unity. If these arguments are accepted it would be an arbitrary distinction to say that Christians are not to evangelize Muslims or Hindus yet they may evangelize Marxists, secular humanists and hedonists. It is not just evangelism of those of other faiths which is under question, but the validity of the whole evangelistic enterprise. Pastoral care, counselling, the administration of the sacraments to the faithful, personal Bible reading and prayer can all be tolerated as valid expressions of privatized religion in a pluralist society such as Britain in the 1990s. Evangelism, however, is inimical to the spirit of pluralism, and always will be.

It has to be said that some attempts at evangelism in Britain have indeed been careless, arrogant, driven by guilt rather than love, badly thought out, and culturally insensitive. William Abraham, an Irishman writing mainly about the American situation, points out how much modern evangelism buys into Western culture's individualism, pragmatism and worship of success:

> On the one side modern culture appears to be deeply opposed to the intellectual content of the Christian gospel, and tends to dismiss it as meaningless and irrelevant. On the other hand, those who are most resolute in their championing of the cause of evangelism are liable to be reactionary or they have themselves succumbed to the acids of modernity.[2]

The prospects for evangelism in the 1990s viewed from this angle look decidedly bleak!

Evangelical Anglicans and evangelism

Over against this, several factors suggest a new vision of evangelism emerging in the church. Many recent studies have highlighted the surprising persistence of faith and search for some non-material 'meaning' to life. Jonathan Sacks, the Chief Rabbi of Great Britain drew attention in his 1990 Reith Lectures to the fact that 'religious attachments remain even in a society in which religious behaviour is measurably in decline'.[3] The spiritual dimension is one of the great fascinations of the 1990s. A desire for an inclusive global and ecological spirituality lies behind much of the New Age movement and moves within Christian theology to embrace and affirm other faiths as expressions of that same spiritual reality. It seems, despite all talk of secularization, that we do not after all live in a post-religious age! Whatever one thinks of the Decade of Evangelism, it has certainly placed the topic on the Church of England's agenda in a way few would have thought possible even in the mid-80s. Many churches around Britain for the first time in years are beginning to consider the question of what evangelism might mean for them. Books on the subject appear frequently, mostly of the 'how to' variety. It is hard to think of a sustained detailed serious and British analysis of the theology of evangelism in recent years,[4] yet despite this, the debate has proceeded vigorously within evangelicalism and several ways of thinking have opened up.

1. *Holistic Evangelism.* In 1984 John Stott wrote:

> One of the most notable features of the worldwide evangelical movement during the last ten to fifteen years has been the recovery of our temporarily mislaid social conscience ... now we are convinced that God has given us social as well as evangelistic responsibilities in his world.[5]

This endorsement by the leading figure in Anglican evangelicalism over the past forty years testifies to a very definite shift in one strand of evangelical thinking on evangelism. Chris Sugden[6] has helpfully charted the development of this approach from the Lausanne Declaration of 1974 through to the Stuttgart declaration of 1987, and shows how for many within evangelicalism, the social context of evangelism has come to be seen as crucial. Evangelism is not simply the proclamation of an unchanging message in all places at all times, but the context in which the gospel is proclaimed 'affects the very proclamation itself'.[7] Within this strand of evangelical thinking, the precise relationship between social responsibility and evangelism is construed in various ways. All the same, it has become increasingly common in evangelical circles to think of evangelism as being integrally related to social responsibility, that the goal of Christian mission is the total transformation of the human condition from one which falls short of God's will for people to one in which they may enjoy liberty and justice in harmony with God.

2. *Power Evangelism.* The 1991 MARC Europe Report, '*Christian*' *England* highlighted the extent to which the numerical growth points of the church in England lie more often than not within churches of a charismatic evangelical persuasion. Many of these churches, within Anglican renewal as well as the 'New Churches' have taken on various forms of the 'power evangelism' associated with John Wimber, the founding pastor of the Vineyard Fellowship in California. This approach grew out of (some would say beyond) the church growth school which although starting in the USA has gained a significant following in Britain. 'Church growth' tries to combine an evangelical understanding of the gospel with insights from the social and behavioural sciences to enable organic numerical growth within churches. 'Power evangelism' uses some of these insights, yet sees evangelism taking place in conjunction not so much with social action, but 'power encounters' where supernatural healings, miracles, and 'words of knowledge' are used as signs of the eschatological kingdom seen in the present age as a kind of preparation for the gospel. Resistance to the Christian gospel is overcome by specific and visible/audible demonstrations of the power and reality of God. In this understanding, evangelism is seen as integrally related to the supernatural display of the power of the Holy Spirit.[8]

3. *Classical Evangelism.* A third significant strand within evangelical Anglican thinking holds to a more classical evangelical understanding of evangelism, that it consists solely of the proclamation of an unchanging message. This approach would tend to be suspicious of too close a link with social action, not denying its appropriateness, but insisting on the absolute priority of proclamation in evangelism, seen basically as 'working for conversions'. Here also is often found more than a little scepticism and even hostility towards the charismatic emphases of 'power evangelism', seeing these as distractions from the main task. Hence a criticism of one of John Wimber's meetings: 'There was no gospel in the so-called evangelistic meeting. The cross of Christ was not central; the atonement not explained; and mankind's need and the provision of redemption not even cursorily treated.'[9] The

stress on clear explanation, on the message of sin, redemption and judgement, the presentation of the intellectual content of the Christian gospel, are the distinctive emphases of this approach.

These three brief pictures are deliberately and necessarily starkly drawn. There are considerable differences of emphasis within the three approaches, and many evangelicals would find themselves hard put to identify clearly with only one of them. They represent a spectrum, rather than three entirely distinct 'camps'.

This quick survey shows on the one hand that evangelicals cannot simply recall the Anglican churches to an evangelical view of evangelism, if only because there are *several* evangelical views of evangelism! On the other hand, it does illustrate the fact that evangelicalism has become a vital forum for lively debate about the meaning and practice of evangelism within the Anglican churches, and surely it is only through such debate that theologically and culturally responsible evangelism can emerge within Anglicanism. One of the main challenges facing evangelical Anglicans over the next decade or two will be that of holding together an increasingly diverse constituency, and this is no less true of its thinking on evangelism. Given the wider situation in both church and society, and the state of play within evangelicalism, the need for such a common theology of evangelism cannot be overestimated.

The theology of evangelism

One feature that the three approaches outlined above have in common is a growing sense that in essence, evangelism is not about 'asking Jesus into my heart', but rather, is fundamentally linked to the kingship or kingdom of God, which has partly come, but is yet to come in its fullness. The holistic approach sees evangelism linked with working for a just society as bringing people to enjoy the full benefits of the kingdom of God.[10] Power evangelism sees 'signs and wonders' as signs of the kingdom,[11] and classical evangelism stresses that to become a Christian is to come under the Lordship, kingship or rule of God.[12] What precisely this kingdom is and how it is manifested is a matter of some debate, yet at least in this concept there is a starting point for developing an understanding of evangelism: *to evangelize is to invite people to come under the rule of God.* [13]

In biblical understanding, evangelism can never be a human programme, or a human initiative, but it begins with a divine decision and a divine idea. From Isaiah's vision in the temple, to Jesus's, 'I must preach the good news of the kingdom of God . . . for I was sent for this purpose' (Luke 4.43), to Paul's understanding that God 'makes his appeal through us' (2 Cor. 5.20), the emphasis is clear that to evangelize is not to start a recruiting drive for church membership, but it is to be a part of God's movement towards the world, the *missio Dei*, which takes its distinctive shape and form from the place where God has made his will and purposes known, the place where his rule comes to us and is made available to us: Jesus Christ.

The theological heart of evangelism is therefore Christology. A high and robust Christology will surely lead to and involve evangelism. If the form of God's address to and action in the world is found in Christ, and the ministry of Christ was to invite people to repent and enter the kingdom of God, then to be a Christian means being caught up with and involved in some way in that same address and action in the present. Conversely, a low and tentative Christology will draw the sting from evangelism. It is highly significant that many works which aim to renounce the necessity of evangelism start at this very point. Keith Ward's *A Vision to Pursue*, in which he sets out his 'conversion' to the need for Christians to disavow their traditional exclusiveness in favour of a search with other religions for a 'convergent spirituality', starts with an analysis of the fallibility of Scripture. This leads him to the meat of his argument, a reinterpretation of the incarnation, so that Jesus becomes 'a human being who is transparent to the divine, rather than . . . a divine being who takes on a human nature'. [14] Similarly, John Hick's *The Second Christianity* starts with a chapter on Jesus in which he concludes that to believe that Jesus is the only sure way to God is to 'misuse the language of personal commitment and turn living religion into dogmatic exclusiveness.' [15]

These writers have seen, correctly, that Christology is the point from which the rest of Christian theology and ministry takes its shape. The argument usually proceeds to the issue of the uniqueness of Jesus, this being denied on the revisionist side and energetically affirmed on the traditionalist (and evangelical) side. Yet it is not only because of its denial of the unique revelatory and salvific status of Jesus that the revisionist approach strikes at the heart of evangelism. It mainly does so because it denies that God addresses or reaches out towards the world and makes himself available in it in any meaningful sense. The movement in such revisions tends to be all the other way: the human search rather than the divine mission. 'Who do you say that I am?': the answer to that question of Jesus will determine whether Anglicanism takes the road opened up by the Decade of Evangelism, or the road along which the revisionists have already begun to walk, eschewing evangelism as a relic from the unenlightened Christian past.

Unfortunately, there is no space here for an adequate analysis of the revisionist views of Christology mentioned above. This has been done elsewhere[16] yet it can be said that the question is not whether Christianity alone holds truth: it is less common now even among evangelicals to find the idea that all other religions are purely demonic imitations of the truth. Many evangelicals also make use of the apologetic argument that those who have not heard of Christ may yet be saved. As Michael Green puts it, 'If they do not rely on their own fancied goodness, but cast themselves on his mercy, they may well be among those who are surprised on the day of judgment to find themselves sheep rather than goats.'[17] Such an argument does not rule out that there may be salvation in other religions, though only through the mediation of Christ.

The real question is this: to revise, or not to revise? If God does not reveal himself in any exclusive or definitive way in Jesus Christ, then evangelism, or anything worth the name, must come to an end. If God does reach out to the world in Jesus Christ, if 'God was in Christ reconciling the world to himself' (2 Cor. 5.19), then evangelism, inviting and urging people to be reconciled to God, is a Christian imperative. The final motive for Christian evangelism is neither simply the command of Jesus, nor a kind of aggressive and jingoistic zeal or jealousy for the name of Christ (Christians would do well to be wary of such language in the light of the excesses justified under similar terms in the church's own history or in militant Islam, for example). Instead it is the inner logic of the movement of God in love and judgement towards the world in Christ. If Jesus Christ discloses the true heart of God in a way nothing or no one else does, then in that heart lies an invitation and the means to come under the kingship of God, and find rest and reality there. To be caught up in that is to find that 'the love of Christ compels us' (2 Cor. 5.14) to call the bluff of twentieth-century secular pluralism, just as the early Christians did with second- and third-century pagan pluralism. That means being committed to extend that same invitation in the present, 'to bring our faith into the public arena, to publish it, to put it at risk in the encounter with other faiths and ideologies in open debate and argument, and in the risky business of discovering what Christian obedience means in radically new circumstances and radically different human cultures.'[18] Evangelism can never truly be an adjunct to Christian life and ministry, precisely because it flows from the very heart of Christian theology: the movement of God towards the world in Christ.

Evangelism and the church

At the outset of this essay it was noted how often Anglicanism has displayed an embarrassment about evangelism which has pushed it on to the fringes of church life. Billy Graham-style campaigns, from the 1950s to 'Mission 89', have increasingly felt the need to tie their efforts in to local churches, yet at the same time illustrate the same tendency to separate the work of evangelism from church life. It remains to point out just two out of many possible important implications which the understanding of evangelism developed above, based on a Christology which speaks of God's movement towards the world, has for the practice and place of evangelism in the church.

1. *The occasion for evangelism.* The New Testament does not abound with exhortations to churches to 'go out and evangelize'. It does contain instructions, for example, to 'make a defence to any one who calls you to account for the hope that is in you' (2 Pet. 3.15). An outsider is intrigued by the strange optimism that a Christian possesses, asks about it, then is told what it means and why it is there. In a simple way this illustrates a common pattern which chimes in with the theological basis for evangelism suggested

above. Effective proclamation of the gospel normally takes place when people see the effect of the presence or rule of God in the life of an individual or community, ask 'What does this mean?', and are then ready to hear the answer, which is the message of Jesus Christ, crucified and risen. Evangelism is the natural consequence of Christology and therefore of life under the rule of God.

As Lesslie Newbigin has pointed out, the same pattern is at work on the day of Pentecost, and continues to be the shape of effective evangelism today:

> Where there is a community whose members are deeply rooted in Christ as their absolute Lord and Savior . . . there will be a challenge by word and behaviour to the ruling powers. As a result there will be conflict and suffering for the Church. Out of that conflict and suffering will arise the questioning which the world puts to the Church.[19]

It is perhaps this very factor that both holistic and power evangelism have to teach the rest of the church. Many may be unhappy with power evangelism as being at odds with Jesus's refusal to give signs to make people believe (Matt. 16.4), and what some see as an incipient dualism. Similarly, holistic evangelism can find itself unhelpfully tied to a provisional and dubious political programme, and can turn Christian ministry into sanctified social work. Nevertheless, the fundamental insight they have in common is that evangelism arises out of the work of God in the world, and follows in the tracks of God: the gospel is proclaimed as the answer to the question, 'What does this mean?' (Acts 2.12). This may help us towards an understanding of the interrelationship and interdependence of social action and proclamation in evangelism. In its most basic form, without deeds (whether works of compassion, the fight for justice or dramatic supernatural encounters) no one listens, but without words (the telling of the story of Christ and the invitation to believe), no one understands.

What I have called classical evangelism preserves the crucial place of proclamation within evangelism. If outsiders are not told the reason for the 'hope that is within' the Christian, the hope for the full coming of the rule of God, in whatever form that hope displays itself, they will never understand it and be able to come to believe it for themselves. Yet to set proclamation over against the need for visible and tangible expressions of the rule of God is nonsense: without deeds no one listens. Similarly it is wrong to suggest that for a church to set up a scheme to help house the homeless in a parish is worthless unless it leads to conversions. Such action may well be part of a church's living out its life under the rule of God. It may be done with the hope that people may ask, 'What does this mean?', yet the work has value in itself as an expression of life under the kingship of God.

Evangelicals have been very good at what John Wimber calls 'programmatic evangelism'. Perhaps the reserve of some Anglo-Catholics and liberals has something of value for evangelicals, if it springs from a desire to let evangelism arise naturally out of the life of the church in which God is present. Planning, organization, gospel outlines all have their place, but if they do not find that place in the context of a community, an individual, or relationships which know what it is to live under the rule of God, and are caught up in God's initiative towards the world, they are likely to bring little fruit.

2. *The status of evangelism.* In 1967 the World Council of Churches produced a report which contained some prophetic ideas about the mission of the church. It identified what it called 'morphological fundamentalism', the tendency of the church to adopt a 'rigid and inflexible attitude towards the *morphe* or structure of the congregation'. The danger is that of perpetuating '"heretical structures", i.e. structures that impede the *missio Dei*'.[20] These are salutary words for the Decade of Evangelism. If evangelism flows naturally and directly from the movement of God towards the world, from Christology and the kingship of God, why do we find it so hard? The answer surely is that churches have a habit of developing ways of acting and thinking which keep the lid firmly on this natural outflow and (to change the metaphor) strangle it at birth. For a church to feel its evangelistic conscience tweaked, and proceed to 'do a bit of evangelism' on the side by organizing a mission, doing some door-to-door visiting, or even to appoint a parish evangelist, is to walk up a blind alley. If evangelism is tacked on to the side of church life, while leaving the essential structures intact, as has often been the case in the Anglican churches, what results is an awkward,

theologically deformed body, storing up for itself much frustration and failure.

Taking evangelism seriously both theologically and ecclesiastically will involve a much more radical look at the way a church works, how its services are planned, how its resources are deployed, how its people are cared for and nurtured, what kind of sermons are preached, and much more. One parish church recently faced a difficult decision. The large and somewhat static mother church had always had two curates, and had recently planted a small but thriving church on a local council estate in the parish. When one curate moved on, the PCC had to choose whether to keep their two curates at the mother church or to take the brave and radical decision to place the new curate in a house on this council estate. They decided for the former: they would 'service' the new church from a safe distance, and keep their two curates where they had always been. To change would have involved sacrifice, pain, cost and inconvenience. Yet it is precisely this kind of imaginative structural change which will need to take place if a church is to keep step with the movement of God in the world, and to keep the invitation to enjoy the rule of God open.

The evangelistic dimension cannot be delegated to a committee and hastily forgotten, but must constantly be present in every decision taken, and in justifying the work of each part of church life. This does not mean that every service becomes self-consciously evangelistic, preaching becomes simplistic or the women's fellowship is closed down because it is not producing converts. To take evangelism seriously is to take the world alongside the church seriously. So, for example, the youth group will need to ask itself, 'Are we addressing the issues faced by the young people of this area? Would outsiders coming into this group find their concerns taken seriously and given an intelligible and genuinely Christian response? Are they likely to experience in the relationships and the concerns addressed the rule of God at work here?'

In normal parish life, most people are brought to faith in Christ not by a demonstration of logical proof but by being persuaded to join the community of those seeking to live under the rule of God, to look at the world from that Christian perspective, and find that it works, it makes sense! For this to happen, people may well need to spend considerable time as part of a church which has evangelism built into its very structures before they come to explicit and conscious faith in Christ. For this, the fuzzy edges between church and community found in most Anglican churches potentially give them a great advantage. Because the Anglican churches do not have rigid membership requirements, it is possible to be a part of Anglican church life for a long time, weighing the options, before deciding which way to turn. If the theological debate on evangelism continues and is taken up by others within Anglicanism, if dioceses and local churches have the insight to discern and courage to implement structural change, the Anglican churches are well placed to bring their philosophical and evangelistic schizophrenia to an end, to let Butler and Wesley shake hands.

Notes

1. K. Ward, *A Vision to Pursue* (London: SCM Press, 1991), p. 173.
2. W. J. Abraham, *The Logic of Evangelism* (London: Hodder & Stoughton, 1989), p. 200.
3. J. Sacks, *The Persistence of Faith* (London: Weidenfeld & Nicolson, 1991), p. 8.
4. On the other side of the Atlantic, W. J. Abraham's book, *The Logic of Evangelism*, makes a stimulating attempt to fill the gap he himself acknowledges. Abraham's outline and suggestions have much to say to the British picture, but there is no equivalent treatment focusing particularly on the Anglican situation. Lesslie Newbigin's work on the gospel and Western culture is the nearest there is to a serious theology of evangelism, and hopefully will spawn a new set of studies in this field.
5. J. R. W. Stott, *Issues Facing Christians Today* (Basingstoke: Marshalls, 1984), p. xi.
6. C. Sugden, 'Evangelicals and Wholistic Evangelism' in V. Samuel and A. Hauser, eds, *Proclaiming Christ in Christ's Way: Studies in Integral Evangelism* (Oxford: Regnum, 1989). See also R. Padilla and C. Sugden, 'How evangelicals endorsed social responsibility', *Texts on Evangelicals and Social Ethics 1974–83* (Nottingham: Grove Books, 1985).
7. Sugden, 'Evangelicals and Wholistic Evangelism', p. 33.
8. See J. Wimber, *Power Evangelism* (London: Hodder & Stoughton, 1985). It is worth noting that John Wimber has since expressed dissatisfaction with this book; a revised edition has since appeared.
9. M. Thompson, 'Spiritual Warfare II' in *John Wimber: Friend or Foe?* (London: St Matthias Press, 1990), p. 20.
10. See for example, C. Sugden, *Radical Discipleship* (Basingstoke: Marshalls,

1981), p. 110: 'Evangelism is making known the evangel, the good news of the kingdom of God as announced and inaugurated by Jesus Christ.'

11. The first chapter of the first version of John Wimber's *Power Evangelism* is entitled 'The Kingdom of God', a foundational concept in his understanding of evangelism. The first part of the revised edition is entitled 'The Kingdom has come'.

12. *Two Ways to Live* (London: St Matthias Press, 1989); a simple gospel presentation often used in this approach begins with 'God is the loving ruler of the world', and invites the addressee to 'submit to Jesus as our ruler'.

13. Abraham's *The Logic of Evangelism* similarly takes the concept of the kingdom of God as the starting point for developing a theology of evangelism.

14. K. Ward, *A Vision to Pursue* (London: SCM Press, 1991), p. 56.

15. J. Hick, *The Second Christianity* (London: SCM Press, 1983), p. 32.

16. For brief and penetrating examples, see A. E. McGrath, 'Resurrection and incarnation: The foundations of Christian faith' in A. Walker, ed., *Different Gospels* (London: Hodder & Stoughton, 1988), and 'Pluralism and the Decade of Evangelism' (*Anvil*, Vol. 9/2, 1992).

17. M. Green, *Evangelism through the Local Church* (London: Hodder & Stoughton, 1990), p. 72.

18. L. Newbigin, *Truth to Tell – The Gospel as Public Truth* (London: SPCK, 1991), pp. 59–60.

19. L. Newbigin, *The Gospel in a Pluralist Society* (London: SPCK, 1989), pp. 136–7.

20. World Council of Churches, *The Church for Others and the Church for the World: The Quest for Structures for Missionary Congregations* (Geneva, 1967), p. 19.

8

Evangelicalism and the Foundations of Ethics

OLIVER O'DONOVAN

How are Christian ethics evangelical? If we are prepared to weigh the words we use, we must understand this question to mean, how does our knowledge about what we are to do make us glad – glad, that is, with the gladness of the gospel?

'Then were the disciples glad,' the evangelist reports, 'when they saw the Lord' (Jn. 20.20). This is what distinguishes evangelical gladness from any other kind of satisfaction that the church, like the rest of humankind, may take in prosperous circumstances: it springs from the resurrection of Jesus. The church was glad, Eusebius reported, when the emperor Constantine hosted a lavish banquet for the bishops who had just concluded the Council of Nicaea, a celebration so glad and so magnificent, the historian commented, 'one might have thought a picture of Christ's kingdom was shadowed forth'. The church had much to celebrate. Like the church in Eastern Europe today, it had emerged with dizzying suddenness from the shadows of persecution into the light of official favour. It had averted, so it seemed, a threatening doctrinal schism. We can hardly suggest it should have felt anything but pleased. Yet we cannot know to what extent its gladness was the true gladness of the church of Jesus Christ; for that depends on whether, and on how, the risen Christ stood in its midst. The object of evangelical joy is Jesus, Jesus vindicated by the Father who would not leave his soul in sheol nor suffer his holy one to see corruption.

We must always state first that the church rejoices quite particularly in *his* resurrection. That would be cause for joy even if

96

there were no implications of a universal kind. Yet we must add that the disciples saw in Jesus's resurrection the resurrection of the whole human race. They believed he was the Son of Man, representing the whole race before God. That his resurrection should be an isolated happening, a personal transaction only, in which he was airlifted out of the life and destiny of human beings, that was inconceivable. If the representative was raised, the race would follow him. It is from the resurrection rather than the cross that St Paul formulates his most famous statement of Christ's representative role: 'Since by man came death, by man came also the resurrection of the dead. As in Adam all die, so in Christ shall all be made alive' (1 Cor. 15.21). This statement then points us further. The resurrection of mankind in Christ is the reversal of that slide from created order into dissolution that began with Adam's disobedience. The resurrection of the race means that we may live, but not merely live in our disordered state but live in a renewed order. Renewal is not a hope for isolated individuals alone; it means participating in a world that has been renewed.

So joy in the resurrection leads us to rejoice in the recovery of creation – but that is not a joy we can experience from a spectator's point of view, but only as participants. Gladness belongs to God's creatures, as glory belongs to the creator. The church is glad when it can take the place assigned to Adam's race within the cosmic order, giving articulate utterance to the rejoicing of the inarticulate elements. This is mankind's 'rational worship', expressing in company with every creature the fact that in Christ's resurrection created order is restored. In the risen Christ both gladness and glory are present: the gladness of the living creature, present and alive to God, and the glory of the God who raised him from the dead. There will be something to be said, too, about the glory of the church; of how mankind is lifted up in Christ to share God's glory at God's right hand. But we need as yet know nothing about that. It is enough that the creature has regained the joy proper to it, greeting the glory of its maker and knowing his energy at work within itself. The early evangelicals brought to Anglican morality a sense, which it had lacked, of the redemptive energy of God, visible in the conversion of individuals and the reconstruction of a broken society. A reflection on evangelical ethics properly finds its point of departure there.

The objectivity of God's work

This glad worship is the central core of the Christian moral attitude, a disposition of the affections and the will which springs from the recognition of God's mighty deeds. Of the affections, first of all; that is, the pleasure we experience when we contemplate what God has done and shown himself to be. Jonathan Edwards, who, if anyone, can be claimed as the moral theorist of the eighteenth century evangelicals, laid a distinctive stress upon the role of 'holy affections', which 'are primarily founded on the loveliness of the moral excellency of divine things'. He described them as a 'sense of heart of spiritual beauty', and as a 'divine taste . . . wherein the mind don't only speculate and behold but relishes and feels' (*Religious Affections* III.3, 4).

Out of the affections come the resolutions of the will. It was a wrongly oriented affection that led the first couple to decide that their own wills should determine their existence. But out of true delight better resolutions of the will may follow. Delight leads to doing and to making; it does not stop short at tasting and enjoying. By doing and making we take the place assigned to us in God's created order, so that his work comes to its completion. Moral goodness, wrote Edwards, is 'that good in beings who have will and choice, whereby, as voluntary agents, they are, and act, as it becomes 'em to be and to act, or so as is most fit, and suitable, and lovely.' Nevertheless our choices spring from our delights; and any deed worth doing has its origin in delight at God's self-disclosure. It is a delight in something *there*, something of God's doing and making that invites our appreciation and joy. Action not founded in appreciation is destructive.

But even to say this much constitutes a protest against a longstanding tendency in Western thought to make a sharp division between knowledge and will. A resolution of the will produces an act; it is doing something, something new that was not in the world before we did it. But how can an act which introduces new reality into the world be conditioned in any way by knowledge of the reality that preceded it? What is the rational fitness that makes us think, 'God has redeemed us, *therefore* let us serve him!'? The apostolic writers constantly move from proclamation to prescription, pivoting on the word 'therefore': what are we to make of this 'therefore'? The formal question, as old as Aristotle, has been revived intensively in modern philosophy, and some have found no logic to connect the 'is' and the 'ought'. We need not quarrel with the modest claim that this logic is not deductive. But not all rational inference is deductive. It is possible to speak of the appropriateness or inappropriateness of given acts to given realities. An act of will may be a *new* element within reality, but it can never be a *dissociated* element. Our behaviour always takes on the character of a response to what was there before, a response that may accept or reject the world into which we act. For Edwards the affections, which at one and the same time discern reality and incline towards it, are the bridge between the rational and the voluntative powers of the human mind.

An evangelical ethics will be on its guard against two mistakes, opposite in their effects though identical in their conception, which springs from the voluntarist separation of the act of will from discernment.

The first mistake is to conceive our action as radical innovation, a kind of repetition of the divine creation *ex nihilo*. We do not confront emptiness when we act; it is not our task to confer form and being upon void. Our creativity is exercised on the basis of God's accomplished acts of creation and redemption. A sharp caution is in place against the fashionable presentation of political involvement as 'making a new and better world'. We ought to see this fascination with world-making as a recurrence of the old Adamic temptation, 'You shall be like God!' A universe waiting to be made, still undetermined, even in the character of its gods! When did such a prospect fail to evoke wild conceptions of human power and destiny? If human action is not worship, it will become, in Yeats's phrase, 'hysterical pride'. Our doing and making (for, of course, we do make things, though not worlds!) must either grasp at unlimited possibilities which, if they really were unlimited, would destroy us, or else it must be the glad acceptance of those defined possibilities that are offered us in what God has made. 'The world is established, it shall never be moved' (Pss. 93.1, 96.10). That is the security which makes us free to act; our doing and our making has its place in that world, and can be fruitful in that world for the exploration and unfolding of that world's mysteries. It is precisely because we do not act into emptiness that

99

it is possible for us to act at all. But acting into a universe of meaning requires a discerning love of that universe and a delight in its meaning.

The second mistake is to think we need a kind of stepping-stone between the truths of the gospel and the action corresponding to them – as though what God has done is not enough to elicit action, but requires to be helped out by a different kind of divine act, a 'command' that will bind our consciences. There is no need for stepping-stones. When we have said, 'Blessed be the God and Father of our Lord Jesus Christ, who has begotten us again to a living hope . . .' we have said all that is necessary to make the conclusion intelligible: 'Therefore gird up your minds and be sober . . .' (1 Pet. 1.3, 13).

This is not meant as a repudiation of the notion of divine command, a notion deeply embedded in biblical ethics. The Scriptures tell us of law-giving at Sinai; and that Jesus gave prescriptive moral teaching to his disciples. Ordinary moral catechesis in the church has often proceeded simply by repeating these commands and the injunctions of the apostles, and in this way it has been able to point both to the event in which the command originated and to the demand now made on the disciple. This was how the nineteenth-century Anglican evangelicals proceeded, and we ought to be very hesitant about saying they did not know their business. They were responding to an earnest religious moralism that seemed to be taken captive by fashion; and in the text of the biblical commands they sought to achieve a measure of biblical objectivity.

Nevertheless, when biblical commands are isolated from their context in the narrative of God's works, the demand they make becomes less, not more intelligible. For a command, once given, becomes a fact of history; once it has discharged its authority into action it is like an exploded firework. The fact that it was issued then does not make it authoritative for all believers at every time. A culture as aware of history as ours is is rightly uncomfortable with the thought that we could be bound by the commands of Jesus to his disciples simply, as it were, by overhearing them.

Yet this hesitation should lead us back to what does bind us, which is the work of God. And the point of the commands is that they give a moral exposition of the response elicited by God's acts of salvation. They draw their authority for us *from* the acts; they do not supply an authority which the acts have somehow failed to supply. Reality is authoritative and action-evoking, and nothing else is. In his acts God has determined the reality that now conditions us; in his commands he has explained what this reality requires of us. That is why in using the prescriptive texts of Scripture for our own deliberations we are expected to be intelligent. Command ethics have a bad name, but it comes from the misuse rather than the proper use of the biblical commands. Commands are to be understood. They witness to a train of thought which takes us back to reality itself. If we have not understood their witness, mere scrupulosity will not teach us how to obey them. Better, certainly, to act in obedience on a partial understanding if we must; but we should never give up the quest for understanding and fall back into merely habitual performance. The application of biblical commands to our own decisions must be thought about; so must their relationship to each other, for the variety of different commands reflects what divine intelligence conceives as a unity, a single integrated purpose for human life in the world. To understand commands together, and not separately, is to understand what Scripture refers to when it speaks of God's 'law'.

The Law

There is something in the moral law which invites us to perceive it as a burden. It is not simply that it is difficult. Some things we must do are difficult, of course; others may be delightfully easy. But even something difficult is not necessarily a burden; it only becomes a burden if a great deal hangs on its success. A crossword puzzle is not a burden, an examination is; yet the crossword puzzle may be very much more difficult than the examination. The burden of morality is that so much *does* depend on how we live; we are responsible for ourselves. The burden of morality is final judgement, that last verdict, hovering over us like a vulture, whether our years on earth have been a waste of time or not. Moral decisions are problems because they confront us anew with our responsibility for ourselves, and stir up new anxieties about what we are doing with our lives. This is the ground occupied by the Pauline discussion of 'the law'.

The effect of God's law, as St Paul saw it, was to 'make sin become more sinful' (Rom. 7.13), which we may paraphrase: to throw responsibility into sharper focus. The Old Testament contained two traditions of evaluating law, each bringing responsibility into focus in a different way. In the Deuteronomic literature and the Law Psalms the law is a solution to our anxiety. It clarifies the questions that have been unclear, dispelling the vague dread that we might, by incautious conduct of ourselves, destroy ourselves. It is a lamp for our feet and a light for our paths (Ps. 119.105). The soul in mortal dread 'pants eagerly' for God's command to 'direct his steps' so that 'evil will win no power' over him (Ps. 119.131, 133). In contrast, the sixth-century prophets, notably Jeremiah and Ezekiel, find that the law has been inadequate to stave off national disaster; it has turned anxiety into guilt. It needs to be given afresh, in a new and spiritually regenerating way. In St Paul's famous discussion of the law in Romans 7 these two strands are woven together. The law is a blessing which has become, in human history and in individual histories, a curse, not because it has changed but because our relation to it has changed. But the change of blessing into curse is part of the wider divine plan which will bring blessing to fulfilment 'apart from law'.

Much of the difficulty of Protestant ethics arose from the bold and creative attempt of Martin Luther to reappropriate this strand of Pauline thinking. In the Catholic tradition the tension between justification 'apart from law' and the task of moral deliberation has not been felt so sharply. Christian ethics has often been expounded as the 'evangelical law', a phrase which has a self-contradictory sound in Protestant ears. Critics of Tridentine Catholicism can complain justly, I think, that the loss of tension meant a loss of something important in the evangelical experience. Yet it is hard to resist the suspicion that Luther screwed up the tension rather further than St Paul ever did. In a fascinating passage from the 1535 Galatians Commentary, Luther says that the medieval distinction between the active and contemplative lives is properly understood as the distinction between law and faith: 'The speculative life should be included in, and directed by the Word of God . . . but that the active life should be sought from the law, which does not grasp Christ' (*WA* 40¹:446). In this the whole of our active existence seems to be cut off from evangelical inspiration.

The Reformed tradition tried to speak more positively about the moral content of the Christian life. Yet the way in which it related morality to salvation was not wholly satisfactory. Calvin's doctrine of the 'third use' of the law, for all that it entered a warning against the threat of antinomianism, still justified Christian ethics in terms of St Paul's law–gospel antithesis, as a burden and a discipline, a lingering memory of the curse of God on sin. This leaves us unable to conceive moral theology as evangelical theology. The moral theologian is allowed to be useful for the Christian life, but only as an irritant. You would not turn to him for news to gladden your heart.

But St Paul speaks also of a 'life in the Spirit', not as a purely interior life but as an active life, and not as a life of formless enthusiasm but as a life with its own order and reason. The task of moral theology is to point to that life and to describe it, celebrating it as the gift of God to mankind. It does not have to speak of bad news set in dialectical opposition to good news; it proclaims the good news in one of its aspects. It traces the form of a life lived in Christ and in the power of the Spirit, and it opens it up to our understanding, so teaching us to rejoice in it. There is, of course, also an ascetic and disciplinary side to moral theology, but it is not primarily an ascetic discipline, just as Christian discipleship itself involves participation in the cross of Christ but is not primarily crucifixion but resurrection.

Thus the gospel restores the blessing of law, as it was formerly conceived in the Psalms and wisdom tradition. The order which God created no longer threatens us. We can discover it as a liberating context for life rather than as a dead weight of condemnation and hopelessness. When St Paul speaks of 'fulfilling the law of Christ' (Gal. 6.2) he points to the transformation of moral demand into something that is by no means 'law' in the sense of condemnation but is still God's given order for our ways. The classic polarization between legalism and antinomianism, the curse of Protestant ethics, springs from a failure to grasp the

moral order *itself* made new in Christ. We do not have to decide
for or against a law intrinsically hostile to evangelical liberty, but
simply embrace 'the perfect law of freedom' (Jas. 1.25).

The struggle for righteousness

The widespread disenchantment with Christian morality in
contemporary Anglicanism has something to do with the false
perception that the church's business with morality is primarily
that of a teacher, not that of an actor. It is always giving moral
counsel, never receiving it. But properly understood the church's
'ethics' (using the word to mean its tradition of reflective *thought*
about morality) is its understanding of the life that it itself has
been given to live. Theological students who think they will study
ethics in order to have something to say, must first learn that
something is being said to them. The moral theologian, too, must
sometimes wonder whether he or she may fight in war or have an
abortion. It is not all worked out for others' benefit!

That said, however, the church does need to preserve its
understanding of the resurrection life as it is lived within its own
fellowship; and it does need to point others, without ambiguity,
towards that resurrection life for which they are destined. The
idea of moral teaching is not to be ignored, merely placed in
context. The resurrection life is integral to the gospel, not a mere
appendix to it, and for this reason must be visible within the
community and, where necessary, defended, as the gospel word
itself may need to be defended. The church cannot, of course,
pretend to maintain, in a world compromised by ambiguity, a pure
witness in which every thought is open to the sun. Nevertheless,
there are some false trails to be marked off, some wrong signposts
to be corrected. And if the church neglects to do this, it neglects to
preach the resurrection in its fulness.

It will not succeed in proclaiming the resurrection, either, if,
whether from misguided Protestant scruples about law or for any
other reason, it is not prepared to manifest the shape of Easter life
in open controversy with untrue values which have come to
dominate society. Here is the point at which it is right to speak of
burden and of suffering, and of the law in its old character of
condemnation. The Christian life, though not primarily a

crucifixion but a resurrection, also involves the conflict of the cross for the sake of resurrection. There can be no holding back from the conflict in which the kingdom of God engages with the principalities and powers. We are called to struggle for righteousness, both personal righteousness and public.

In the struggle for public right there are dangers. We may come to identify the gospel with some secular or other outlook with which we happen to strike up a provisional alliance in objecting to some evil, or with some programme of reform to which we may become uncritically attached. These dangers can be countered only by preaching the gospel in its wholeness, for the gospel always transcends the particular controversial engagements and programmes with which the church at any time may find itself involved. They are a serious menace only if the church is tending to lose its purchase on the gospel itself, if the host of Israel is actually about to be seduced by the gods of the Canaanites against whom it is sent to war. That such a seduction, never an outright impossibility, can at times become a terrible likelihood, we cannot deny. But we will not call the church to faithfulness by withdrawing it from its struggle and counselling contentment with its own self-contained existence.

In the eighteenth and nineteenth centuries evangelical Anglicans were prominent in public struggle, and the impact that they made on the care of destitute children, colonial slavery and the treatment of prisoners is a part of British social history. It earned them enemies – Charles Dickens's sneers about the 'cant' of prisoners' welfare stick unpleasantly in the mind. And however it may look to us today, it was not obvious to contemporaries that their struggles were all 'progressive'. Opposition to slavery, especially, seemed like conservative resistance to the new global economic order, the great 'colonial system'. But that was beside the point. It is not given to anyone to choose whether the struggle he or she will undertake shall be 'radical' or 'conservative'. The application of these words is determined by fashion; by what contemporaries happen to think about progress, and indeed by whether they happen to think about it at all. Those conditions can change overnight, as many left-leaning causes have recently discovered to their cost. The desire to engage in fashionable struggle is simply a desire to adopt the posture without paying the price of conflict with society. The struggle of the cross is one which takes its calling solely from the joy that is set before it, the pattern of the resurrection life in its completeness.

But it could hardly be said too forcefully that the church's struggle, as indeed its whole life, must point forward to the redemption of mankind as a whole. The church in controversy *against* mankind will cease to be the church of Jesus Christ if it is not, at the same time, struggling *for* mankind. Any cause that does not envisage the healing of all Adam's children will be sectarian, a mean tussle on the part of one group to triumph over another. Yet to struggle in an open spirit, resisting adversaries but not closing the doors of love and hope against them, is difficult. The church stands at the heart of the contradiction of the end-time, with the new order restored in Christ on one side and the old array of rebellion, chaos and death on the other. It has to live in the gladness of the resurrection while it still suffers the hostility of the cross. It must die and live with Christ at the same moment, experiencing resurrection in the very place of defeat. To sustain the tension can be so demanding that the church may well be tempted to withdraw from it into the purely temporal and provisional stratagems of struggle, consolidating gains and extenuating losses, aiming to outwit rather than to win over, to negotiate its way round challenges rather than to meet them.

How, then, may it recall that its struggle is against the principalities and powers, that its triumph is assured and final, and that its victories are held in trust for all mankind? How can it sustain its Easter joy in conflict, as an eschatological sign of the resurrection of the human race? It can do so by forgiving its enemies.

During the last three years we have reflected constantly upon events in Eastern Europe, on the new assertion of freedom there, not least the freedom to worship, and on the collapse of government fashioned out of deceit and oppression. The church has had a particularly close interest in this revolution, as a beneficiary and as an influence upon it. Yet, like other revolutions, it began in joy and continued in anger. Delight gave it its first impulse, but recrimination was the engine that carried it forward. In God, the Psalms tell us, anger is short-lived and gives way to joy; but with us the reverse is the case, and joy erodes too quickly into grim resentment. Our joy lacks staying-power to separate us from the haunting memory of the past and to chart our way into the future; so we rely on indignation to do the job.

But Jesus said, 'There will be joy in heaven over one sinner who repents' (Luke 15.7). A revolution driven by indignation will have little interest in repentance. If there is one thing you didn't want to be, during the last years and months in ex-communist Europe, it was a reforming Communist, who began to develop doubts and to look for changes. People like that were swept aside in the search for a radical break with the past. But in heaven there is more joy over one apparatchik who has come to suspect the truth about the regime than there is over ninety-nine liberal dissidents. Can the church identify with the joy of God? Can it greet its old opponent with delight, because he, too, is free from the powers of spiritual wickedness against which its struggle was directed? Only so can it be the church of Jesus Christ, the community of his resurrection. Perhaps if we look back at the bishops in Nicaea with that question in our minds, the whole Constantinian revolution will appear in a new light.

9

Evangelicalism and
Social Ethics

NIGEL BIGGAR

In the early 1970s evangelical interest in social ethics was reawakened. After at least two generations of neglect, partly attributable to a reaction against the substitution of social reform for religious conversion by the social gospel movement, the political unrest of the late 1960s provoked evangelicals on both sides of the Atlantic to ask themselves how Christian faith could respond to the burning questions of the day.[1] To a certain extent, they were thereby resuming the social concern of some of their nineteenth-century forbears. Some of these, most famously William Wilberforce and Anthony Ashley Cooper, the 7th Earl of Shaftesbury, had been deeply distressed by certain social ills of their time and campaigned tirelessly for their alleviation. Many others, however, were inclined to take a laissez-faire attitude to economic and social suffering, seeing it as expressive of divine justice and conducive to repentance;[2] and even the interventionists sought the alleviation of symptoms rather than the reform of their structural causes. So, although current evangelical interest in social problems does comprise the resumption of an earlier tradition of concern, it also represents a new departure. For contemporary evangelicals are much more inclined than their Victorian predecessors to conceive of economic and social life as the proper objects of divine redemption – as is indicated by their appeal to the incarnation as the basis of Christian social involvement,[3] and by their emphasis on the social nature of the kingdom of God.[4] They are also more inclined to be critical of given social institutions and, correlatively, to take their thinking about social life right back to the level of basic principles.

108

Among those evangelicals who have written in the field of social ethics during the past twenty years, many have been members of the Anglican Communion. It is perfectly possible to speak, therefore, of an evangelical contribution to social ethics in the Anglican church. But it is much less possible to speak of an *Anglican* evangelical contribution, because what evangelicals have written about social ethics has seldom been distinctively Anglican.

In one sense, this is a rather odd comment to make, for how could one expect evangelical social ethics to be Anglican when the *Anglican* tradition of social ethics (represented by the likes of F. D. Maurice, B. F. Westcott, Charles Gore, and William Temple) lies firmly in the Catholic wing of the church? Moreover, whether or not a body of thought is Anglican is in itself hardly an issue of importance. The important issue is surely whether it is true, incisive, and illuminating. In certain respects, then, it may well be best that social ethics be *less* 'Anglican'; that is, that it should not replicate the weaknesses of the Anglican tradition of social ethics to date. However, in other respects it may be the case that evangelical social ethics should be more Anglican in the sense of maintaining and developing certain valuable elements that the Anglican tradition has incorporated.

Anglican social ethics are the better for the evangelical contributions made to them; but those evangelical contributions would be the better for becoming more Anglican. That is the thesis of this chapter. Here follows the argument.

The evangelical contribution

Anglican social ethics benefit from evangelical work in at least five ways:

The first way is through the characteristically close attention that evangelicals pay to relevant material in the Bible. In recent years, for example, C. J. H. Wright has produced a thorough account of the social ethics of the Old Testament,[5] and Richard Longenecker has done the same (though less thoroughly) for the New Testament.[6] Quite what value such biblical work has for contemporary social ethics is, of course, a controversial matter. On the one hand, some have argued that the Bible as a whole or the New Testament in particular cannot be of any help at all to

modern ethical endeavours, either because of the cultural abyss
which separates 'modernity' from the biblical world view or
because of the basis of Jesus' ethics in a discredited eschatology. It
is fair to say, however, that neither of these arguments has carried
the field of Anglican social ethics. Certainly, its most eminent
contemporary representative, R. H. Preston, holds that the Bible
does have an ethical role to play, albeit a more limited one than
evangelicals would tend to espouse.[7] On the other hand, if some
have underrated the value of the Bible for contemporary social
ethics, others have overrated it. I shall discuss and criticize shortly
the tendency of some evangelicals to suppose (or, at least, to
imply) that biblical exegesis is virtually sufficient for the
construction of a Christian social ethic. Here it is my purpose to
say what I believe that the ethical value of biblical exegesis is, not
what it is not. Minimally, I believe it to be that of making available
for contemporary appropriation wisdom about the social good life
which has been formed within theological visions of reality that
belong to the same family – the same tradition – as our own. The
point here is simply that those trying to interpret the meaning of
the Christian vision of reality for social life today would be foolish
not to avail themselves of whatever valid insights can be gleaned
from those who have gone before, including those who stand in the
biblical part of the Christian tradition.

Unfortunately, many Anglican social ethicists, no doubt in
reaction against the naivete of ethical biblicism, neglect the biblical
part of the tradition entirely, as if the only way of denying that the
Bible says everything were to pretend that it says nothing. One of
the most important services, therefore, that evangelicals perform
for Anglican social ethics is that of demonstrating that close
attention to the Bible, even if it is not sufficient for the construction
of a social ethic, nevertheless yields incisive insights into the
principles of social well-being, and striking instances of it, that
can be fruitful for contemporary thinking. For example, there is
the insight that the *raison d'être* of any kind of social authority,
including political authority, is to support and enable those subject
to it. This is implied in the Old Testament by the use of 'shepherd'
as a metaphor for king; and in the gospels it is implied by the
theme of the first becoming last, stated in Jesus's response to the

political ambitiousness of James and John (Matt. 20.25–7), and shown in his washing of the disciples' feet.[8]

Another, related insight is that political, social, and economic life should be so organized as to enable genuine, small-scale communities to hold as much power and exercise as much responsibility as possible. This was embodied in the original allocation of inalienable portions of the land to Israelite 'clans' or tribal sub-units (Num. 26, 34; Josh. 13–19) and defended by the laws concerning redemption procedures and the Jubilee (Deut. 15; Lev. 25). A further, related insight is that those who hold political power should hold it lightly and be willing, when appropriate, to surrender it to others. This is strikingly embodied in the decision of the apostles, reported in Acts 6, to heal a rift in the Jerusalem church caused by a racially discriminate abuse of power by transferring that power entirely into the hands of the aggrieved. The distribution of food from the common fund had become corrupted by ethnic prejudice (Acts 6.1). Widows who were culturally Greek ('the Hellenists', RSV) were being neglected, because the distribution was in the hands of Aramaic-speakers who were culturally Palestinian ('the Hebrews', RSV). The apostles' decision was to give charge of the distribution to seven men who, judging by their names (Stephen, Philip, Prochorus, Nicanor, Timon, Parmenas, and Nicolaus), were ethnic Greeks.

A second important contribution that evangelicals make to Anglican social ethics is that of insisting that it be true to its basic theological convictions – that it be careful to consider the social ethical implications of the Christian vision of reality. Some recent products of Anglican social thinking have failed to do this, and have proceeded by using ethical concepts – e.g. of justice or community – that have not been theologically baptized.[9] Such failure of theological criticism is attributable partly to the faith of the British Enlightenment in common moral sense, partly to a Thomistic confidence in the power of natural reason to grasp the natural moral law, partly to the desire to be intelligible outside the walls of the Christian church, and partly to the adoption of liberation theological method.

In contending for the theological appropriation of social ethical

111

concepts, I do not mean to imply that common moral sense is necessarily mistaken or that natural reason's grasp is invariably weak. Unless one holds that the sinful corruption of human being is absolute apart from faith in Christ, and that the effective reign of Christ Ascendant (the redeeming presence of his Spirit) is strictly confined to social circles that are self-consciously 'Christian' – positions that wide experience of non-Christian conduct makes it hard to sustain – then one should expect to find elements of common moral sense, or intuitions and conclusions of natural moral reason, that are congruent with Christian convictions. Indeed, throughout the history of Christian ethics this is an expectation that has been amply fulfilled. The high regard of Thomas Aquinas for the political theory of Aristotle is, of course, famous. Less well known, perhaps, is Calvin's admiration for the political philosophy of Cicero (*Institutes* IV, xx).

Nevertheless, if Christians are bound to treat common moral sense with respect, they are equally bound to make their respect critical, to assess what is taken for moral wisdom outside the church in terms of Christian convictions about the human condition and the human good. If Christians have a duty to handle the moral opinions of their non-Christian fellows with openness and respect, they have no less of a duty to take seriously the moral implications of their own, not entirely common, vision of reality.

Nor, in contending for a measure of theological rigour in social ethics, do I wish to depreciate the desire to be intelligible to outsiders. If Christians really care for their non-Christian fellows, then they will not rest easy with theological jargon. They will strive to find familiar words by which to *communicate* what needs to be said. But this does not mean that they should renounce the use of their own language altogether. For if they are to communicate something new, then they must be allowed to say something different; and they cannot say anything different if they speak in entirely familiar terms. If Christians were to jettison their own language, they could say nothing different, shed no light, offer no help, tell no good news. So the church's task is a delicate one. For on the one hand, it must speak in terms sufficiently familiar to be understood; but on the other hand, it must use familiar terms in unfamiliar ways if it wants to say something interesting. The commendable desire to win broad support for a

Christian vision of social life needs to be balanced by an equal desire to offer a social vision that is, in fact, Christian.

Evangelical insistence that social ethics be theologically rigorous does contradict less sophisticated versions of liberation theological method. In over-reaction against what is taken to be the politically abstract and strictly deductive method of traditional Western theology, some advocates of liberation theology – Anglicans among them[10] – propose a theological method that simply takes its cue from the economic, social, and political situation – or, more precisely, from the moral demands implicit in it. The major problem with this is that it repeats the mistake of the social gospel movement in making theology merely the rationalization of a set of prior moral commitments. In the opening sentence of *A Theology for the Social Gospel* (Nashville, TN: Abingdon Press, 1945), Walter Rauschenbusch was quite candid about marshalling theology in support of socialism: 'We have a social gospel. We need a systematic theology large enough to match it and vital enough to back it.'

Surely, however, theological convictions should be allowed to criticize, and so to help determine, praxis. It may well be that theological endeavour in the past has not been sufficiently attentive to the moral claims made upon it by its political context, and that theologians today should let political reality impinge more directly upon what they do and how they do it. Nevertheless, theology – and that includes theological social ethics – needs to move dialectically back and forth between the particular situation in which it is lodged and its basic convictions about reality, and not merely monolinearly from praxis to theory. Otherwise, it will simply serve to shield a given set of political commitments from criticism.

A third way in which evangelicals make a positive contribution to Anglican social ethics is in helping to resist any tendency for the social dimension to swallow up the religious one.[11] Such a tendency is present in certain reaches of liberation theology, as it used to be in the social gospel movement.[12] Take, for example, Enrique Dussel's book, *Ethics and Community* (1988), where we are told that 'offense to God is *always and antecedently* an act of domination committed against one's brother or sister' (my

113

emphasis), and that 'there is no such thing as a religious sin that is not a political or economic sin . . .'; and where discussion of the 'reign of God' in Christian life focuses almost entirely on the social state of 'being together with others'. (It is true that Dussel describes this 'being together' as being 'with God', but since no account is given of the distinction and relationship between human community and communion with God, it appears that 'God' is but another name for community.)

Against such social reductionism, evangelicals contend that the relationship between the human creature and God is distinct, albeit not separate, from her relationships with other creatures. Therefore, in addition to right conduct toward one's fellows, there is also the matter of right conduct toward God. In addition to the duties of social justice, there are also the duties of prayer. Indeed, the fulfilment of the one depends on the fulfilment of the other.

Evangelical insistence upon the importance for social health of the discipline and cultivation of spiritual life is not, of course, unique in Anglican circles. It has long been one of the distinctive virtues of the Catholic Anglican tradition of social ethics that it places the disciplines of worship and prayer at the heart of social endeavour. So, while evangelicals might tend to conceive the spiritual life in more pietistic terms – although, in fact, evangelical piety has become somewhat more 'Catholic' in recent years[13] – they nevertheless share common cause on this matter with other Anglicans.

Allied to this affirmation of the importance of spiritual life as distinct from social life is an affirmation of the importance of social ethos as distinct from social structures.[14] In addition to the quality of political, social, and economic institutions, laws, policies, and conventions, there is also the matter of the values that are prevalent in a society and which shape the ways in which people regard and treat one another. There is the matter of personal convictions and attitudes. It is perfectly true, of course, that certain kinds of social structure encourage certain kinds of social ethos. The Roman Catholics are right: laws do have a morally educative and formative effect. But social structures do not *determine* social ethos. Different people in similar social situations can behave in widely different ways. Moreover, the promotion of a certain ethos can sometimes have a (re)formative impact upon social structures. Certainly, this seems to have been St Paul's assumption when he wrote to Philemon about his runaway slave, Onesimus. In his letter Paul made no direct assault on the institution of slavery. Indeed, in promising to return Onesimus to his master he paid his formal respects to it. At the same time, however, he appealed strongly to Philemon to receive his slave back as 'a beloved brother' – and to do so freely (Philem. 14). It is hard to imagine how the institution of slavery could remain untouched by an ethos in which master treats slave as 'a beloved brother'. And it is hard to imagine that St Paul supposed that it would.

Evangelical resistance to the notion that the creation of social well-being is merely a matter of structural engineering is an expression of the traditional evangelical conviction of the importance of individual responsibility and personal conversion, both religious and moral. It serves to remind the church that its social vocation is not fulfilled in the lending or withholding of support to or from certain laws and policies. For in addition to that, there is the more obscure and subtle task of promoting salutary social values, attitudes, and practices by eloquent and intelligent word and, more important, by eloquent and beautiful demonstration.

A fifth contribution that evangelicals are making to social ethics in the Anglican Communion – and the final one in our list – comes in the form of constructive work of high standard. In *Thine is the Kingdom* (1984), for example, Paul Marshall has provided a theology of political life which, although not as full as it might have been, is nevertheless systematic and perceptive. In *Economics Today: a Christian Critique* (1989) Donald Hay has written a Christian account of economic theory which ranks among the best that Anglicans of any stripe have produced. And in *Peace and Certainty: a Theological Essay on Deterrence* (1989), Oliver O'Donovan has offered an analysis of the theory of nuclear deterrence at a characteristic level of sophistication that has few Anglican equals.

Becoming more Anglican

So much for what evangelicals are bringing to Anglican social ethics. Now, as I move toward a conclusion, I propose three ways in which evangelical social ethics might do well to become more Anglican.

First of all, evangelicals might serve their cause better by ceasing to describe their social ethics as simply 'biblical'. In practice most are wise enough to know that the biblical text does not yield a systematic social ethic in any direct fashion. And most are sufficiently historically critical to be aware of the Bible's theological and ethical diversity, and to know that it offers the social ethicist a somewhat disparate collection of materials, composed in different times and places and in different forms (theological, legal, casuistic, narrative). But evangelicals still tend to be shy of acknowledging the logical implication of this fact: namely, that social ethics cannot merely be received from the Bible – it has to be *created* out of it. Like any branch of theology, social ethics is a rational construct. It necessarily involves making judgements about the ethical meanings of particular texts and then placing those meanings in a coherent whole that is far more than the sum of all that those particular texts have furnished. There is no choice between taking social ethics from the Bible and building it by the exercise of human reason: the first simply cannot be done except by way of the second. So the choice is never between 'biblical' ethics and 'rational' ethics, but only between 'rational' ethics that strive to make sense of what the biblical authors were talking about and those that do not – that is, between faithful and unfaithful moral reasoning. The emphasis here on the *creation* or *construction* of a Christian ethic out of the Bible should not be understood as recommending a kind of wilful and arbitrary plundering of the text. Not at all. What is being recommended is construction in obedience to the enduring moral truths that the Bible furnishes. But the point that is being pressed here is that this obedience involves more than just a repetition of what is given in the Bible, more even than the explication of what is logically implicit there. It also involves the creation of *new* concepts and rules by the imaginative use of reason. That is why I think that, by describing their social ethics as simply 'biblical', evangelicals risk

116

obscuring the extent to which the exercise of human reason is necessarily involved in what they do, and they encourage other Anglicans to dismiss what they do as naively biblicist. It would therefore be to their advantage to adopt a higher and more overt – a more Anglican – respect for reason.

Second, in claiming to be doing simply 'biblical' ethics, evangelicals obscure the extent to which their rational organization of biblical material draws from the post-biblical traditions of the church. Primarily, of course, it is through the Reformed tradition that evangelicals read Scripture. Nowadays, however, they are more ecumenical in their search for moral wisdom: in *Issues Facing Christians Today*, for example, John Stott quotes approvingly from William Temple, Reinhold Niebuhr, Nikolai Berdyaev, Vatican II, and Pope John Paul II. Nevertheless, he (like others) tends to underscore the 'biblical' character of his ethics and underplay the formative influence of 'tradition', thereby implying a methodology that does not accurately correspond to the method actually employed. If evangelicals were to recognize more fully the extent to which tradition necessarily informs their ethical appropriation of the Bible, they would perhaps find themselves more at liberty to exploit the rich resources provided by almost 2000 years of post-biblical Christian reflection on social life as they seek to make sense of, and develop, the Bible's ethical import. It could well be fruitful, for example, to consider the Roman Catholic concept of 'subsidiarity', according to which it is the state's proper role to enable and empower the family, as a helpful representation and development of the Old Testament's concern that political authority should uphold the maximal devolution of power to the clan. Our Christian predecessors were certainly not infallible, but sometimes they did accurately grasp the ethical point that a biblical text is trying to make. And, if that is so, it only makes sense that we learn from their labours. Evangelical social ethics would serve itself better by adopting a higher and more over – a more Anglican – respect for tradition.

Finally, evangelical social ethics would do well to adopt a more ready, Anglican willingness to engage with secular ideas and to enter into secular debates. Much (though not all) of what evangelicals have written in recent years has been published by evangelical houses and directed at an evangelical readership. That, of course, has not been inappropriate during a period when evangelical social ethics has been preoccupied with trying to get its bearings and stake out its base-camp. Now, however, the time may have come to move out more boldly into the surrounding territory.

Notes

1. For a fuller account of the causes of evangelical neglect of social problems earlier this century, see John Stott, *Issues Facing Christians Today* (Basingstoke: Marshalls, 1984), pp. 2–10.
2. See Boyd Hilton, *The Age of Atonement: The Influence of Evangelicalism on Social and Economic Thought, 1785–1865* (Oxford: Oxford University Press, 1988).
3. See, for example, John Gladwin, *God's People in God's World. Biblical Motives for Social Involvement* (Leicester: Inter-Varsity Press, 1979), pp. 30, 100; David Sheppard, *Bias to the Poor* (London: Hodder & Stoughton, 1984), pp. 10, 196; Stott, *Issues Facing Christians Today*, p. 21.
4. See, for example, Stott, *Issues Facing Christians Today*, pp. 22–3.
5. His account comes in two versions, one directed at a lay readership, *Living as the People of God: The Relevance of Old Testament Ethics* (Leicester: Inter-Varsity Press, 1983), the other in a more academic direction, *God's People in God's Land: Family, Land, and Property in the Old Testament* (Exeter: Paternoster, 1990).
6. Richard N. Longenecker, *New Testament Social Ethics for Today* (Grand Rapids, MI: Eerdmans, 1984).
7. See, for example, R. H. Preston, 'The Bible in the Modern World', *Bulletin of the John Rylands Library of Manchester*, 59/1 (Autumn 1976), p. 173; *Religion and the Ambiguities of Capitalism* (London: SCM Press, 1991), pp. 96–103.
8. The political import of this biblical text has long been widely recognized. It was the custom of monarchs in many European countries to wash the feet of those in receipt of their alms on Maundy Thursday. Unfortunately, this deeply Christian gesture was abandoned by the British monarchy toward the end of the seventeenth century.
9. See, for example, Nigel Biggar, *Theological Politics*, Latimer Studies 29–30 (Oxford: Latimer House, 1988) for a critique of *Faith in the City*, the Report of the Archbishop of Canterbury's Commission on Urban Priority Areas (London: Church House Publishing, 1985); and 'Any News of the Social Good?', *Theology*, XCI/744 (Nov. 1988) for a critique

of *Changing Britain: Social Diversity and Moral Unity*, The Board for Social Responsibility of the General Synod of the Church of England (London: Church House Publishing, 1987).

10. See, for example, two essays in *Theology in the City: A Theological Response to 'Faith in the City'* (London: SPCK, 1989): Anthony Harvey's 'Introduction: an Alternative Theology?', pp. 1–14, and Barney Pityana's 'Toward a Black Theology for Britain', pp. 98–113.

11. See, for example, Nigel Biggar, 'Showing the Gospel in Social Praxis', *Anvil* 8/1 (1991), pp. 8, 10–12.

12. In Rauschenbusch's *A Theology for the Social Gospel* there is no discussion of the spiritual disciplines of prayer and worship, and in the chapter on the sacraments, baptism and the Lord's supper are given an exclusively social significance. We are told, for example, that baptism was originally 'not a ritual act of individual salvation but an act of dedication to a religious and social movement' (p. 198); and that in inaugurating the Lord's supper, Jesus intended to create 'an act of loyalty which would serve to keep memory and fidelity alive' (p. 202).

13. As witness the affirmation by the National Evangelical Anglican Congress in 1967 of the liturgical centrality of the parish communion (see Philip Crowe, ed., *Keele '67* NEAC Statement (London: Falcon, 1967), and the development of interest among evangelicals in spiritual direction.

14. See Brian Griffiths, *The Creation of Wealth* (London: Hodder & Stoughton, 1984), pp. 34–9, 117–23; Biggar, *Theological Politics*, pp. 16–21.

119

10

Evangelicalism and Economic Issues

DONALD HAY

Relations between church and state in England in the 1980s were marked by strong public disagreements between the Church of England and the Conservative government about the objectives and conduct of economic policy. Two incidents may be recalled. The first was the publication in 1985 of *Faith in the City*, the Report of the Archbishop of Canterbury's Commission on Urban Priority Areas, which according to newspaper reports had been described as 'Marxist' by one cabinet minister. The second was the critical response from the Chairman and Secretary of the Board of Social Responsibility of the General Synod to Mrs Thatcher's address to the Church of Scotland Assembly in 1988 in which she had sought to provide a Christian moral defence of her policies. I have a postcard, dating from the mid-80s, a photograph of a hoarding in London advertising an ITV Credo programme on 'the government and the church': the poster depicts Mrs Thatcher administering a spanking to Archbishop Runcie, whom she has over her knee like a naughty child.

Responses within evangelical Anglicanism to the disagreements between church and state have been varied. Some would adopt the Lutheran view that church and state have separate callings under God, and that the Church of England should stick to its task of preaching the gospel and teaching Christian virtues, leaving the politicians to get on with their responsibilities for governing the country. Others would not deny the church a voice on economic issues, but fear that the church has become hopelessly infected with left-wing ideas,[1] or that it has simply failed to comprehend

120

the Christian basis for Conservative policies.[2] Others would broadly endorse the church's critique of those policies.[3] Such a variety of responses was not perhaps unexpected, given the differences of view that had emerged at the National Evangelical Anglican Congress in 1977, resulting in two alternative statements in the section on 'Power in our Democracy'.

In this chapter I cannot attempt to resolve these differences of views among evangelical Anglicans. Rather my concern is to ask what might constitute a distinctive evangelical contribution to social ethics for economic issues, and whether the material which has been published in the last fifteen years or so has begun to make such a contribution. The context in which these questions are asked is one in which there is a well established Anglican tradition of social theology, which determines both the methods of working of bodies like the Board for Social Responsibility, and, to some extent, the content of Anglican reports on social issues.

The method is the 'middle axioms' approach, of which R. H. Preston has been the most persuasive expositor in recent years.[4] Preston traces the approach to the work of J. H. Oldham, but it is apparent that the method owes a great deal of its popularity to William Temple's *Christianity and Social Order*, which was first published in 1942 (though Temple never uses the term 'middle axioms'). Preston defines the method as follows:

> In brief, middle axioms are an attempt to proceed from the basic ethical stance deriving from a theological or philosophical world view to the realm of the empirical by seeing if there is a consensus among those with *relevant experience* of the matter under discussion (both 'experts' and 'lay' folk) as to the broad moral issue raised, and the *general direction* in which social change should be worked for, without getting as far as *detailed* policies. [Italics in the original.][5]

This approach is very evident in the method of working of the Board for Social Responsibility (and of the Archbishop's Commission on Urban Priority Areas), not least when economic issues are under discussion.[6] It should be evident from Preston's definition that the approach is a means to relate the ethics of the city of God (or kingdom of God) to those of the secular city (the kingdoms of this world). Hence the need both to draw ethical insights from the Christian faith (both Bible and doctrine, as interpreted by the church) and to have a professional understanding of how the world works (in this case secular economics and politics). The approach describes a practical procedure for doing social ethics, rather than an abstract method of moral reasoning (which makes the term 'middle axioms' with its connotations of logical deduction particularly inappropriate, as Preston admits).

The Christian contribution to the procedure arises, according to Preston,[7] by a process of discernment, which is '. . . achieved by putting one's understanding of human life, drawn ultimately from the Biblical witness to Jesus Christ, alongside a diagnosis of what is going on today'. He obviously believes that it should be possible to reach agreement on middle axioms with those of other faiths or of no faith at all.[8] This seems to be part of his general belief that the Christian doctrinal or ethical input to the process should be latent rather than explicit. In principle, middle axioms will look different for each issue under consideration, since the process of discernment involves interaction with the facts. The links to theological or ethical materials will not necessarily be obvious.

Clearly, much will depend on the content of the theological and ethical material which the Christian participant brings to the process. Preston is generally very cautious about defining this material too closely. However in *Church and Society in the Late Twentieth Century: The Economic and Political Task*, he gives a brief treatment. He follows the precedent of Temple in distinguishing primary ethical principles based on fundamental Christian principles, e.g. human beings, made in the image of God, are vicegerents of the created order; the fact of human sinfulness implies that economic and political systems cannot assume human goodness, rather the reverse. He then moves on to secondary principles that have more direct application to economic and political issues, though the transition from the primary principles is far from being closely argued. The core of his secondary principles[9] is as follows: (a) the basic equality of human beings before God is more important than the things in which they are unequal; (b) an emphasis on human solidarity and community over against individualism; (c) concern for the poor and

122

disadvantaged; (d) the dignity of human beings requires that they should participate in decisions which affect them as workers and citizens; (e) the sinfulness of human beings requires that there should be checks on the abuse of power, whether economic or political; (f) the state not only has the negative role of restraining disorder and wrong doing, but also a positive role of creating and encouraging institutions, structures and social conventions which facilitate human flourishing in the sense of (a) to (e) above. It should also be noted that principles (a) to (c) have been adduced by Preston to justify the creation of a welfare state in the market economies.[10] These principles, or principles very like them, are frequently alluded to and developed in the theological or 'ethical' chapters of Board for Social Responsibility reports, and there is little doubt that they represent the mainstream of Anglican social theology. In the post-war period, Preston is the most distinguished and consistent contributor to this tradition.

How then does this method for doing social ethics work out in practice, for example in the Reports of the Board for Social Responsibility? One observation is that although the reports bring together much useful material covering a particular economic or social issue in Britain, explicit interaction with Christian principles or theology to produce genuine 'middle axioms' is far from common. This is not to say that the reports lack prescriptive content: they often have quite a number of recommendations to make. But that only compounds the problem: confronted with a prescription with which he or she disagrees, a reader of the report has no access to the process which produced it. Furthermore, the method also seems to preclude any rigorous development of Christian economic and social ethics: since the precise contribution is obscured by the particularities of each application, it is difficult to judge whether a consistent set of principles is being applied.

What has gone wrong? One possibility is that the whole procedure is defective: it focuses too much on the *process* of interaction between theologians and experts, and pays too little attention to the *content* of that interaction. A second possibility is that the theological input to the process is too weak and imprecise to affect the substance of the discussion: indeed, if an objective is to come up with recommendations which will be acceptable to people of other faiths or no faith at all, then the lack of specific

Christian content is easily explicable. A third possibility is that the procedure makes quite insufficient allowance for the secular presuppositions of economic 'experts'. The theologians may be too respectful of their methods and expertise, and are not able to challenge the basis for the 'facts' and arguments which those experts will feed in. There is a particular danger if an expert has an ideological axe to grind.

Given this context, the issue we have to address is whether evangelical Anglicans can contribute effectively to the development of theological ethics for economic life. The first point to note is that whereas before about 1975 it would have been difficult to identify any substantial writing on economics by evangelicals, since 1975 a very considerable literature has developed.[11] Books have been published by Brian Griffiths (*Morality and the Market Place*, 1982 and *The Creation of Wealth*, 1984), Alan Storkey (*Transforming Economics*, 1986), and myself (*Economics Today: A Christian Critique*, 1989), addressing a wide range of economic issues from an evangelical standpoint. In *Making Unemployment Work* (1985), Michael Moynagh has written a more popular book on the problem of unemployment in the UK. *Rich Christians in an Age of Hunger* (new ed. 1984), Ron Sider's work on international economic justice, has been widely read in evangelical circles. The Jubilee Centre at Cambridge, under the directorship of Michael Schluter, has produced an extensive set of papers on theological and biblical ethics for economic life, as well as developing research and policy initiatives on such issues as debt and Sunday trading.[12] Other contributions have been published in the Grove Ethical Series.[13] Nigel Biggar contributed an incisive theological critique of *Faith in the City*.[14] The Association of Christian Economists, whose members are academic and research economists mainly of an evangelical persuasion, has become more active since 1985, holding an annual study meeting and publishing a samizdat style journal twice-yearly.[15] Whatever judgement one makes about the quality of individual contributions to this literature, the number and relative sophistication of published works is in marked contrast with the period before 1975. In what follows we will attempt to delineate the main features with respect to method and content.

The general approach of these writers is not dissimilar to the approach described above. Typically there is an appeal to theological insights which furnish Christian principles for economic life. These derivative social principles are then allowed to interact with economic issues, informed by a careful understanding of modern economic analysis, to arrive at general prescriptions concerning economic policies and institutions without detailed formulation of policy (unless the writer happens to be an economist with the appropriate expertise to suggest policy options). How then does the evangelical Anglican contribution differ?

First, there is a much clearer statement of the theological justification for the method. A clear distinction is drawn between the people of God and the secular city. The principles for economic life which are advanced are those that should fashion the common life of the people of God. They can therefore presuppose a degree of commitment to following Christ, though members of the church remain sinful people. These principles stand as a witness and as a warning to secular economics, that the way the world is is not the way God would have it to be. In the process of interaction between Christian principles for economic life and the ordering of secular economies, the fact of human sinfulness forces us to look for second best implementation of those principles in policies and institutions. There is no hope of attaining the kingdom of heaven in a secular society. The Christian economist should hold fast to the vision of what God prescribes for economic life, but be pragmatic in the application of that vision. As part of that application, an important role is assigned to the political authorities, whose task, under God, is to restrain evil and injustice, and to promote the conditions for human flourishing.

Second, as might be expected, evangelicals give close attention to biblical materials in developing their principles for economic life. We should note immediately that Anglican social theology has repeatedly criticized the use of the Bible in this way.[16] It is therefore important to spell out how the Bible has been used in recent writings by evangelical Anglicans. The first point to note is that, despite accusations by liberal critics, there is *no* reliance on proof texts which are mechanically applied to complex social issues. On the contrary there is an attempt to evaluate the diversity of the biblical materials to see what insights they furnish, when taken as a whole, for the understanding of economic life.

The most obvious difficulty is that there is enormous cultural distance between the biblical material and the problems of a modern economy. One part of the solution to this difficulty is to look for the principles that are implicit in the material, and which have significance independent of the particular context of the biblical text. For example, the detailed provisions of the Old Testament law obviously relate to a primitive rural society,[17] but they also reflect principles of economic organization that are significant in very different economic and cultural situations, such as the need to provide every family with a stake in economic life, the priority of work over social security, and the obligation of the rich to lift the poor out of their poverty and reinstate them in society. The other part of the solution is to set the principles *within* a general theological framework which includes the themes of creation, fall, judgement, the Noachic covenant, and the people of God, which are clearly universal and not culture specific.

All of this presupposes that the biblical materials do indeed furnish us with a consistent set of principles for economic life, despite the diversity of literatures and cultures reflected in its text. A theological basis for such a presupposition is that the Bible bears witness to a consistent God, and it would indeed be strange if it turned out to be full of contradictions. A more pragmatic stance is to try to see whether a consistent set of principles can in practice be derived. One significant fact about the evangelical literature noted above is that there has in fact been a high degree of agreement on the basic principles. Obviously the provisionality of these principles needs to be stressed, and they need to be further refined and developed, but the extent of agreement is encouraging.

Third, evangelical writers are committed to the view that the biblical material is authoritative, and that it controls the *content* in the process of doing social ethics. The *process* will still be interactive between Christian faith and the economic issue under consideration; indeed the search for a second best will inevitably require careful consideration of the economic context. But the Christian principles should also inform the way in which the economic issue is described and analysed. The idea of a value-free economic science, which can give an objective description of the real economy, needs careful qualification.[18] The philosophical basis of economics is rationalist and utilitarian, and this has a considerable impact on both the presentation of analysis and the policy options which economists suggest.

Fourth, a particular strength in the evangelical contribution is that much of it comes from those who are or have been practising economists. The 'middle axiom' method has relied on interaction between Christian theologians and secular 'experts', and this inevitably generates problems of communication. Christian economists are much better placed to appreciate the contribution of theology, and to relate it to their economic analysis in a detailed and appropriate manner.

What kind of principles have emerged from this evangelical Anglican reflection on Scripture? Despite differences of emphasis between writers, there is agreement on a number of key issues.[19] The starting points are particular aspects of biblical doctrines of human nature and of creation. The paradigm introduced by Wright[20] is helpful here. Imagine a triangle of relationships with God at the apex, the human race and the created order at the other two corners. God relates to the human race by entering into covenant relationships. These relationships are distorted and broken by human sin and disobedience. God relates to the created order by sustaining it, having brought it into existence. However the main focus of the present discussion is on the 'horizontal' relationships, between members of the human race, and between the human race and the created order. On the first, we note that human beings were made to live in communities of love and respect, in which marriage and the family were primary, but by no means the only social units. The people of God, in both the Old and New Testaments, are a model of human community based on love and mutual support. On the second relationship, that between humanity and the created order, the biblical picture is that of the human race as God's vicegerents responsible for the stewardship of the created order, enjoined not to waste or destroy what God has provided, but to use these resources, together with our God-given talents and initiative, to produce goods and services to minister to human needs.

From these starting points, and reflecting on a wide range of biblical materials, more specific principles for economic life can be derived. First, the human race is called, both individually and corporately, to exercise stewardship, or, to use more contemporary language, to 'create wealth', that is to produce the goods we need for our existence.[21] This stewardship of the created order is something to which every person is called to contribute their resources and talents. In practical terms, that means that each person should have a stake in the economic life of the community. But stewardship also requires that individuals be made responsible both in the sense that they determine how their resources are to be used, and that they be held accountable for their stewardship. That has implications for the definition of property rights, as Brian Griffiths has particularly emphasized,[22] and for the ways in which productive enterprises are organized and controlled.

A second set of principles relates to human work. Work is seen to be fundamental to human nature, both an obligation and a right. It is an obligation, in that stewardship requires everyone to contribute their gifts and talents (though subject to their right to take rest one day in seven). It is a right, in that useful work contributes to a person's sense of self-worth and dignity. Work is also a social activity, in which people co-operate as joint stewards of resources. These principles have application to issues concerning the organization of work and employment (e.g. the rights of workers, employment legislation, health and safety at work) and employment and unemployment (particularly the evil which unemployment represents).

A third set of principles concerns the distribution of goods. Each individual (and family) has the right to have basic needs met. There is no *right* to consume more, particularly if others' basic needs are not being met. There is an obligation on the rich to help the poor. These principles have a particular application to questions of income distribution and social security. The first defence against poverty should be productive work; those who are not able to work should be generously supported. But a social security system should never be used as an excuse for tolerating unemployment, and should be designed to provide incentives to work, as far as possible.

A fourth set of principles concerns the role of the political authorities. They should seek to encourage economic institutions that are most likely to be conducive to the principles outlined above, primarily through a framework of law. They should be seen to be acting to redress perceived injustices in the economic life of society through, for instance, policies to deal with involuntary unemployment. They should play an 'enabling' role by providing a focus and an institutional framework for responsible communal endeavour. In particular, decentralized administration to maximize local participation (for instance in the implementation of social security) is preferable to a more efficient but centralized scheme. (This is equivalent to the 'principle of subsidiarity' developed by Roman Catholic moral theologians.)

Having identified areas of agreement, it should be noted that there are a number of less settled issues. One is the role of 'private property', which is vigorously defended by Griffiths.[23] The question is how far the biblical concept of stewardship responsibilities is consistent with the Roman law doctrine of private property which is usually taken to be definitive in the Western capitalist economies. The second is how far 'equality' should be a Christian principle. Equality of opportunity is implicit in the division of the land in the Old Testament: equality of material goods seems to be implied by Paul's exhortation to the Corinthian church (2 Cor. 8.13–14). A third issue is that of the prohibition of usury in the Old Testament. This issue is particularly interesting as an example of the interaction between an economic problem and theological reflection in the development of derivative social principles. The Jubilee Centre has been researching for some years the problem of debt in Britain.[24] This has required a re-evaluation of the Old Testament ban on interest with a much more positive appraisal of its significance for an advanced economy.[25] A fourth issue concerns the role of government in economic life, and the weight to be given to the safeguarding of economic freedoms. How far do the political authorities have a right to intervene in the exercise of stewardship responsibilities by an individual, when, for example, resources are being wasted, or the environment is being destroyed?

It is also important to note that despite considerable agreement on biblical principles for economic life, there appear to be wide divergences of view when it comes to specific policy questions. For example, a comparison of Brian Griffiths's views with those of

Alan Storkey reveals considerable disagreement. Griffiths, who was a senior policy adviser to Mrs Thatcher, uses the biblical principles to support monetarist policies for Britain. Storkey's conclusions are more supportive of interventionist policies to deal with unemployment. This divergence may reflect no more than a certain immaturity of evangelical Anglican thought in this area. Much of the key literature is very recent, and there remains a need for critical reflection and exploration of differences between the main contributors (and between evangelicals and those who represent the established traditions of Anglican social theology). However, some of the divergences may be explained by the unsettled state of economic analysis, when it comes to policy prescriptions. For example, there may be agreement that unemployment is a grave social evil, but disagreement (among economists) as to the main causes of unemployment and as to the best policies to deal with it. Furthermore, there may be difficult issues about policy priorities on which the biblical principles give no guidance. A more generous social security system, for example, may be a disincentive to job seeking among the unemployed, and a disincentive to entrepreneurs, who face higher personal taxation. The lesson to be learned from these difficulties is that the process of mediating between biblical principles for economic life and the realities of the economy is unlikely to be straightforward. Our understanding is at best incomplete, and in any case a fallen secular economy is unlikely to be particularly amenable to the implementation of Christian ideals.

What of the future of evangelical Anglican ethics for economic life? The divergences outlined in the previous paragraph form an essential first part of the agenda. In addition, there are three areas where a major evangelical Anglican contribution from economists is urgently required. The first is the ecological crisis, where a proper analysis involves cross-disciplinary work between environmental scientists, economists and ethicists.[26] The second is North-South issues (trade, aid and development strategies).[27] The third is an evaluation of the organizations that contribute to the economic (and social) fabric of society – the family, the business enterprise, financial institutions, intermediate organizations and voluntary societies. Storkey has put this area firmly on the agenda, and it needs more work.[28] A final agenda item is a greater commitment to involvement in policy issues. The Jubilee Centre has shown how it can be done in its work on Sunday trading and debt. Evangelical Anglicans need to learn from their example, and to support their work as it develops.

Notes

1. See R. Tingle, *Another Gospel?* (London: Christian Studies Centre, 1988), D. Anderson, ed., *The Kindness that Kills: The Churches' Simplistic Response to Complex Social Issues* (London: SPCK, 1984).
2. B. Griffiths, *Monetarism and Morality* (London: Centre for Policy Studies, 1985).
3. Prebendary John Gladwin, who was Secretary to the Board for Social Responsibility, and co-signatory of the response to Mrs Thatcher's speech to the Church of Scotland Assembly, is an evangelical Anglican, who was previously Director of the Shaftesbury Project (now incorporated in Christian Impact).
4. R. H. Preston, *Church and Society in the Late Twentieth Century: The Economic and Political Task* (London: SCM Press, 1983). See especially appendix 2, 'Middle Axioms in Christian Social Ethics'.
5. R. H. Preston, 'Introduction. Thirty Five Years Later; 1941–76', an introductory essay in a reprinting of W. Temple, *Christianity and Social Order* (London: Penguin, 1976), p. 8.
6. See, for example, Board for Social Responsibility of the General Synod, *Work and the Future* (London: CIO, 1979); *Perspectives on Economics* (London: CIO, 1984); *Not Just for the Poor: Christian Perspectives on the Welfare State* (London: CIO, 1986) and *Faith in the City* (London: CIO, 1985).
7. R. H. Preston, *Church and Society in the Late Twentieth Century*, pp. 104–5.
8. R. H. Preston, *Church and Society in the Late Twentieth Century*, p. 106.
9. Other sources are R. H. Preston, *Religion and the Persistence of Capitalism* (London: SCM Press, 1979), pp. 48–9, and *Religion and the Ambiguities of Capitalism* (London: SCM Press, 1991), p. 65. It should be emphasized that Preston himself does not give a systematic exposition of Christian principles for economic life, so the list in the text is deduced from various of his writings.
10. R. H. Preston, *Church and Society in the Late Twentieth Century*, pp. 123–5.
11. The listing of contributions which follows in the text is not intended to be exhaustive.
12. A list of publications and working papers is available from The Jubilee Centre, 3 Hooper Street, Cambridge, CB1 2NZ.

13. Grove Books Limited, Bramcote, Notts, NG9 3DS.
14. N. Biggar, *Theological Politics* (Oxford: Latimer House, 1988).
15. Details from Dr A. Henley, Keynes College, The University, Canterbury, CT2 7NP.
16. R. H. Preston has been a particularly trenchant critic. See for examples: 'From the Bible to the modern world: a problem for ecumenical ethics' in R. H. Preston, *Explorations in Theology 9* (London: SCM Press, 1981) and R. H. Preston, 'Review of Donald A. Hay, *Economics Today: A Christian Critique*', *Journal of Theological Studies 1990*, vol. 41, pp. 792–800.
17. See C. J. H. Wright, *Living as the People of God* (Leicester: Inter-Varsity Press, 1983). This book has been particularly helpful in the interpretation of economic aspects of the Old Testament law.
18. See D. A. Hay, *Economics Today: A Christian Critique* (Leicester: Inter-Varsity Press, 1989), chapter 3.
19. See in particular, A. Storkey, *Transforming Economics* (London: SPCK, 1986), chapter 5; D. A. Hay, *Economics Today*, chapter 2, section 2; B. Griffiths, *Morality and the Market Place* (London: Hodder & Stoughton, 1982), chapter 3; B. Griffiths, *The Creation of Wealth* (London: Hodder & Stoughton, 1984), chapter 3. The material in Storkey is a brief summary of a much fuller treatment in J. P. Tiemstra et al., *Reforming Economics: Calvinist Studies in Methods and Institutions*, Toronto Studies in Theology vol. 48 (Edwin Mellen Press, 1990).
20. C. J. H. Wright, *Living as the People of God*, especially chapter 4.
21. In R. Harries, *Is There a Gospel for the Rich?* (London: Mowbrays, 1992), the author lists (p. 77) the principles for economic life that are derived in my *Economics Today*, and then comments, 'There is no mention there of wealth creation', seeking to set my views in opposition to those of Brian Griffiths. I did not use the term 'creation of wealth', because by the late 1980s it had strong political connotations, and because in formal economic analysis the term is not well defined. Griffiths defines the term as follows: 'Wealth creation is the value added during the production process'. That is precisely what I prefer to describe as the stewardship responsibility to use the resources of creation to provide for human existence. On this point, at least, there is no disagreement between Griffiths and myself.
22. B. Griffiths, *Morality and the Market Place*, pp. 92–4.
23. B. Griffiths, *The Creation of Wealth*, pp. 56–8.
24. See A. Hartropp, ed., *Families in Debt* (Cambridge: Jubilee Centre, 1988), and Jubilee Policy Group, *Escaping the Debt Trap: The Problem of Consumer Credit and Debt in Britain Today* (Cambridge: Jubilee Centre, 1991).
25. See P. Mills, *Interest in Interest: The Old Testament Ban on Interest and its Implications for Today* (Cambridge: Jubilee Centre, 1989).
26. See D. A. Hay, *Economics Today*, chapter 8, and D. A. Hay, 'Christians in the Global Greenhouse' (*Tyndale Bulletin*, 1990, vol. 41), pp. 109–27.

27. See D. A. Hay, *Economics Today*, chapter Seven.
28. See A. Storkey, *Transforming Economics*. See also D. A. Hay, 'The Public Joint Stock Company: Blessing or Curse?' (*Bulletin of the Association of Christian Economists*, No. 8, 1989), pp. 19–47, and M. Schluter and R. Clements, *Reactivating the Extended Family: From Biblical Norms to Public Policy in Britain* (Cambridge: Jubilee Centre, 1986).

11

Evangelicalism and the Gender Issue

VERA SINTON

People come in two kinds, and if English is your mother tongue you cannot talk about someone for long without selecting a pronoun, male or female. The nursery child, poring over picture books and excitedly adding words to a growing vocabulary, quickly learns to distinguish the difference. If language makes the task important, physical factors make it easy. Even with the most distinctive differences covered up and plenty of overlap in the range of height, weight, length of hair or pitch of voice for men and women, there are enough clues in most cases for the choice to be easy. We can distinguish men from women. If all the visual signs are ambiguous, in the last analysis nowadays we can order a genetic test. Biology has revealed that as well as the spectrum of hormonal differences between male and female there are the discrete alternatives, XX or XY chromosomes, controlling the gender of every tiny cell in the body.

Psychological differences – can they be defined?

One of the fastest growing areas of research and reflection today is the field of gender studies. Serious bookshops have reorganized their shelves to give space to the subject. Much of the work involves going back over areas of psychology and sociology, viewing the data from a perspective that values women's experience and women's concerns equally with those of men. In the process there is a new willingness to attempt to articulate what the differences may be. Women are well aware of ways in which the descriptions of gender differences have operated against them in the past. Men are commonly seen as rational, independent, fitted for public leadership by their objectivity and sense of justice. Women are correspondingly described as emotional, dependent, subjective in their decision-making and well equipped to be care-givers especially in relation to the young and the vulnerable. Such attempts at gender definition have usually been accompanied by an assumption that the attributes ranked as 'male' are of more worth in the public realm, though the 'female' ones have their place within the private sphere of home and family.

A major task of the women's movement has been to chip away at stereotypes which limit the opportunities offered to women. All the qualities mentioned above may be found in various proportions in men or in women. The particular mix for any man or woman will be the result of a combination of genetic factors for that individual, and socialization within his or her culture. Almost all professions in our society now have experience of employing women. It is increasingly obvious that it is impossible to draw up a job description for which women applicants *per se* would be unsuitable on mental and emotional grounds. The physical differences which encouraged role specialization in the past are diminishing in significance in rich countries. With high technology tools hardly anyone works to the limit of their physical strength. The availability of contraception and an overpopulated world means most Western women spend a much smaller proportion of their adult lives in pregnancy and nurture of babies. These are real changes unlikely to go away unless there is global economic collapse.

Separation or connection – a bias in development?

So the major clamour of women today is for equal opportunity to use their talents and be assessed without the prejudice which so quickly creeps in with any descriptive model of gender types. But at the same time the hunch that there are distinctive emphases for the sexes remains; if true, it is dangerous to ignore it. Men have a long head start over women in describing what is normality or maturity for a human being, and if men have a bias towards certain qualities and away from others more favoured by women, then women as a group will always be judged to be the inferior sex. A famous study on the development of moral understanding in women and men by C. Gilligan was sparked off by the finding of her colleague L. Kohlberg that women were 'failing' to reach 'the highest stages of moral development'.[1] The assumption was that a formal and abstract concept of morality as the understanding of rights and rules is better and more mature than a more contextual and narrative focus on responsibility and relationships. Gilligan's own study assumed that parity of maturity could go with differences of emphasis in these areas. She invited, for instance, men and women students to write brief stories about pictures they had been shown. Some were of people in situations of intimacy and some in more impersonal situations of achievement or isolation. She found a higher incidence of fantasies of violence in the stories written by the men, a result unlikely to surprise; she also claimed a noticeable difference in the source of the violent feelings. The men tended to project violence into the situations of personal intimacy, the women into those of competitive achievement. A growing number of women writers are following Gilligan in exploring gender differences on the model of a bias towards separation or towards connection.

Film evidence made a few decades ago showing the stages of anxiety, protest and deep depression experienced by an infant suddenly separated from its parent tore the hearts of those who saw it. It increased the attention that was already being paid to the role of bonding between a baby and a primary parental figure, usually the mother. The experience of receiving reliable care and loving attention lays the foundations of love and trust and a sense of well-being. Then the child begins to move and explore. In gradually phased experiences of separation and reconnection it learns that it is a self relating to others. By the age of about three a typical boy learns he is not going to grow up to be like the powerful and nurturing mother. He has to be like a father who may well be a more absent and abstract role-model. A girl receives a reassuring message that all she has to do is stick close and model femininity on mother. Already there is subtle encouragement for the woman to remain comfortable with close connection and for the man to strike out on an independent course but with some of his underlying fears about relationships unresolved.[2]

Areas of evangelical agreement

Until recently there has been little engagement by evangelical thinkers with the field of gender studies. Snide references to feminists and a highly defensive stance towards the disciplines of psychology and sociology are common in the writings of mostly male theologians and biblical commentators. Among evangelical Anglicans the battle over the ordination of women has brought the subject reluctantly into the open arena and it is clear that there is as much disagreement over the issue as there is within every party grouping in Anglicanism. As the reaction to the November 1992 decision of the Church of England to ordain women to the priesthood indicates, the division can be intense and painful. It is, therefore, helpful to remind ourselves that there are also hugely significant areas of agreement which should not be despised.

First, despite occasional lapses in tone on both sides, evangelicals are united in seeing human gender differences as something to affirm and celebrate. Male and female were created in God's own image and all that God created was very good; a great deal of emphasis is given in the evangelical tradition to the creation account of Genesis 1 which underlines that gender differences are significant and good.

Second, we are equally united in placing a high value on our common humanity. Evangelical spirituality lays great stress on a personal relationship with God. It robustly denies any priestly class with privileged access to God, whose prayers or holiness are of more significance than those of other Christians. Any person male or female, any race or social class can be born again of the Spirit of God, be baptized into the body of Christ, be an evangelist, a servant of Christ and begin to be transformed into the likeness of Jesus. Most of the teaching of Jesus and of the apostles is about character, which is assumed to be common to all humanity. Love, caring tenderness, strength in the face of opposition, humility, concern for truth, wise words in a dilemma, burning indignation about the oppression of the weak; these and many similar qualities are the fruit of Christian character, the treasure which all God's people store up in heaven as they grow in Christlikeness in their daily lives on earth. To affirm the spiritual equality of all human beings is not to utter some irrelevant pious cliché. It is to open up a source of inner wealth, a sense of joyful opportunity and a space for thankfulness which is potentially limitless – and available to men and to women.

Authority and subordination – crucial disagreement

But if evangelicals are united in their affirmation of spiritual equality and biological difference they are thoroughly divided in their assessment of how these affect the social relationships between the sexes. The issue is stated and debated in well-worn terms. Is the biological polarity matched by a psychological polarity reflecting the Creator's intention that the relationship of men and women in marriage and in the church should be one of leadership and authority by men and submission on the part of women? Or does the male domination and female subordination, which we know from experience, belong to the disorder of a fallen world with which the Christian community has to wrestle while at the same time giving witness to the equality which was God's original and ultimate intention?

In approaching ethical questions the evangelical tradition places a very high value on the commands of God as clear imperatives that can be read by an individual directly from the pages of Scripture and applied to the circumstances of his or her life and obeyed. God has spoken, we hear the divine voice and we obey. What is Psalm 119 but twenty-two stanzas of sixteen lines repeating over and over again the Psalmist's determination to take in the commands of God and to keep them? Much of the biblical material where women are visible and distinguished from men is in narrative form. We see Eve making choices in a garden, Sarah becoming the mother of Isaac and of Israel, Deborah making the decisive judgements for the nation, Ruth setting out with Naomi, Huldah advising Josiah, Jesus in dialogue with Martha. A condensed story line lies somewhere behind the affectionate greetings Paul sends to an array of women colleagues. The way in which such passages are noticed and commented on by preachers and writers sends very important signals to women about their identity and value in the church.

A divine command or matter of interpretation?

For many evangelical readers of the Scriptures, however, such material pales into insignificance beside a few clear and applicable New Testament commands: 'I do not permit a woman to teach or have authority over a man. She must be silent' (1 Tim. 2.12) or, 'Wives, submit to your husbands as is fitting in the Lord' (Col. 3.18). I have all too often heard men, slightly embarrassed or firmly defiant, preach sermons on these texts which feel hopelessly unreal. They are not addressing the lives of their congregation or looking seriously at the questions women are asking. Male authority to teach religious truth and female subordination in marriage and in the church is clothed with the aura of divine mystery; fallen minds may not understand or like it, runs one evangelical line, but if it is commanded in Scripture we need to obey in order to live healthy and happy lives in the will of God. Roger Beckwith sums up the position succinctly: 'Examples in the Bible are also "written for our learning", but are not necessarily for direct imitation; doctrines illuminate the reasons for commands and prohibitions; but what are most relevant are the commands and prohibitions themselves.'

I have written elsewhere about the development of evangelical ethics from the 1950s, where the emphasis was on the divine command and the individual, through the 60s and 70s, which saw the rise of more comprehensive social ethics based on theological themes.[4] I find that during a one year course on ethics most evangelical ordinands travel the same path. They start out with a strong orientation towards the Bible as a rule book and find that with that approach it is silent on many issues where they expect guidance and that it speaks with a polyphony of contradictory or paradoxical voices on others. It becomes clear that they are (and always have been) bringing a doctrinal framework to bear. They are going round the well known interpretative spiral: their theology is being used to help them make decisions about the application of individual texts while at the same time the texts are sometimes challenging the theology. ('Theology' here includes not only statements about the character and activity of God and Christ but also beliefs about what it means to be human and to be male or female in a world created by God but disordered by sin and evil.)

There are six passages in the epistles which address specific exhortations to women and might therefore come in the category of divine commands or prohibitions about their role (1 Cor. 11.2–16, 14.34–5; Eph. 5.22–33; Col. 3.18; 1 Tim. 2.9–15 and 1 Pet. 3.1–6). They should cover their heads in public worship, ask questions of their husbands at home rather than speaking in the congregation, be submissive or obedient to their husbands, refrain from teaching and having authority over men. There is a long history in the Christian church of these being read as rules to be applied literally to women for all time. It is salutary to remember that only in the twentieth century has there been a widespread review of this approach in the various branches of the Christian church. But though the revised view is recent it has taken root well. Those evangelical Anglicans who retain the view that subordination of women to men is an abiding Christian social structure, no longer base their argument on what many would call a 'fundamentalist' use of the texts in the epistles, as divine commands. Instead, all sides look at the passages in context, assume that there are cultural differences in the situation facing the church today and try to discern underlying principles which can be applied today. What they do not do is to dismiss the passages as the prejudiced and irrelevant ramblings of a patriarchal apostle. Much of the distrust among evangelicals of feminist theology is a reaction to this kind of approach.

Parallels with slavery and monarchy – time for change?

If the texts concerning the behaviour of women are viewed with respect, one thing that becomes clear is that they form part of a wider body of material where submission and orderliness are the themes. The call for wives to order themselves under their husbands is one example of the call for various categories of people to submit or obey in relevant relationships. How was the freedom of the one who had been baptized in the name of Jesus, whether Jew or Greek, male or female, slave or free, to be lived out in the hierarchical structures of the day? Slaves now have a higher loyalty to Christ and he gives them the dignity of choosing also to submit to masters, though within the institution of slavery they

140

have still in effect little choice. Similarly citizens to Caesar, wives to husbands.

Cultures change, however, and the church often struggles to understand the Word of God in the light of the new situation. It was a painful battle for our forefathers to reach agreement that the apostolic teaching did not confirm for all time the divine right of kings. Wilberforce and the original Anglican evangelicals fought a similar battle for the abolition of slavery. Is it the task of our generation to bury any divine sanction for the subordination of women?

Head as leader – the link with creation

The majority of evangelical writers resist this historical argument with its parallelism between democracy, employment relations and the gender issue. They argue that there is a crucial difference based on two things. The first is the way the narrative about Eve is referred to in the course of the argument in 1 Corinthians 11 and 1 Timothy 2. The other is the Pauline metaphor describing the relationship of husband and wife as head and body. They believe that the symbolism of 'head' denotes authority and rule, and accept that the epistles are giving us a paradigm of how to deduce timeless truth about masculinity and femininity from the narrative details that Adam was formed before Eve and the woman was the one deceived by the snake. They conclude that the New Testament writings confirm that God has ordered creation to include a hierarchy of relationships. Men should take the lead.

Once these two assumptions have been accepted it is easy to fit everything else in Scripture into the framework they create. From the entry of sin in Genesis 3 a destructive imbalance of dominance by men and dependence by women is acknowledged as part of the pain of a sinful world. Patriarchal household structures prevail in Israel and in the Gentile world of the early church. The women we meet in the story live their lives within those constraints. Jesus treats women as spiritual equals with men. This, as already observed, is an enormously liberating foundation for the Christian community. But Jesus makes no direct pronouncement on whether a social hierarchy is part of God's creation plan or not. It is not obvious to men who read the text with the 'head equals boss' interpretation in their minds that there is any time bomb ticking away within God's revelation to challenge their easy acceptance that it is women's destiny to be subordinate to men.

If there is truth in the idea that the bias in male and female lies in the area of separation and connection as discussed earlier, then the model would predict that men would have a natural bias towards defining 'head' in a hierarchical manner. On this theory, the male is more likely to see the one flesh relationship as a threatening close encounter which needs to be regulated by designating a final authority. Women in recent decades have been drawing attention to the evidence that 'head' frequently carries the connotations of 'source'.[5] The ordered relationship of Father and Son in the doctrine of the Trinity was understood to be about the unity and mutual interdependence of the Persons which were safeguarded by the Father being the source of the Son (and Spirit). It does not undermine the authority or restrict the role of the Son.

The word 'authority' occurs in 1 Corinthians 11.10 and the subordinationist interpretation takes it to refer to a woman under male authority. An equally feasible exegesis is that Paul is arguing for the Christian woman's authority to be a worshipper in her own right but counterbalances this freedom with the need to maintain unity and interdependence of husband and wife symbolized by the closeness of the biological metaphor of head and body, with the extra overtones of the ordered relationship of head as source. A flurry of research around the Hebrew and Greek uses of 'head' is currently underway.

If the significance of the 'head-body' metaphor as a basis for excluding women from leadership is now being rigorously challenged, so too are the deductions being made from Paul's allusions to the narrative in the garden. Without this New Testament factor few today would attempt an argument that Genesis 2 teaches a subordinationist view of women. David Atkinson, for example, writes: 'The removal of a piece of the man in order to create the woman implies that from now on neither is complete without the other. The man needs the woman for his wholeness and the woman needs the man for hers. Each is equal in need in relation to the other. Nothing could make clearer the complementarity and equality of the sexes.'[6]

The tradition of interpreting the story with a subordinationist slant has deep roots. The second report by the House of Bishops to General Synod on the ordination of women in 1988 examined four of the details: the man created first, woman created from his rib, the woman described as 'helper', the woman brought to the man and named by her. On all these events in the story the bishops were divided between interpretations implying authority for Adam and ones which did not. More recently in the Statement by the House of Bishops on *Issues in Human Sexuality* a categorical sentence appeared: 'In Genesis 2 the man, as a royal figure, has authority over the woman, demonstrated in his giving her a name'.[7] The evidence against this has been well presented by a number of evangelical writers such as Atkinson and Mary Hayter.[8] It is one of the details on which the New Testament makes no comment. What is interesting is how persistently male commentators latch on to a theory which assumes naming to be the impersonal activity of gaining power over an object. Women are more likely to consider naming as the starting point of a relationship. A large proportion of the examples of naming in the Bible are of mothers naming their sons at the moment of birth and bonding.

The case for subordination as a creation design is hanging as an enormous weight on the thread of the Pauline argument. Is it a strong enough cord? It assumes that Paul was following modern evangelical guidelines for intepreting the Old Testament when there is plenty of evidence that he did not. We would be very cautious about deriving covenantal principles about the institution of slavery ('Arabs shall be slaves') from Paul's use of the Hagar and Sarah story in Galatians 4. The parallel with the concept of a creation ordinance about Adam and Eve is too close for comfort. There is a good case for seeing the use of Genesis 2 in 1 Timothy 2 as similarly allegorical. Eve formed after Adam was not instructed in the command of God in the story and was deceived. She is a type of Christian women, newly brought into the covenant but not yet instructed, who need to learn rather than to exercise their new freedom by teaching the men. (There are quite a number of variations of this type of exegesis of the passage.)

Prejudice – a serious ethical issue?

An important factor in the 'good case' for selecting such an interpretation is that the ones which use the more solemn concept of a creation ordinance have difficulty avoiding the implication that the narrative implies that women are more easily deceived than men. There is a moral issue here involving truthfulness and the effects of prejudice which has seldom been taken seriously enough in evangelical writings. The influential Grove Ethics series produced a booklet early on (1978) with the rather coy title, *Are Women People Too*? It has been notably silent since on truth and justice issues affecting women. The Men, Women and God project operating from St Peter's, Vere Street, recently had an imaginative roadshow to try and put such issues on the agenda, backed up by the writings of Elaine Storkey and Kathy Keay.[9]

So some evangelical Anglicans have found that when they probed the familiar and apparently strong case for a 'creation ordinance' of male authority and female subordination, it crumbled away. For them the biblical passages exhorting submission and quiet learning still carry an abiding message of the importance of good order and close relationships between the sexes in the church; marriages of mutual submission and loving self-giving, realism not asceticism about sexual needs, sensitivity to the prevailing culture, a leadership that has been properly instructed and is equipped to teach. They do not include any permanent ban on women occupying leadership roles for which they have been trained, their gifts having been duly recognized by the church. The apostles used moral arguments which included the need for the church to be seen to behave well in relation to the moral values of the society in which it was set; such arguments point in our day to removing the restrictions on the ministry of women.

A larger number of evangelical Anglicans, I suspect, retain the view which links male leadership to creation. They reject the suggestion that a change of attitude to women is the challenge of this century, similar to the change of attitude to slavery needed two centuries ago. Among these there is a middle group of people who favour the ordination of women to the priesthood. They limit their application of headship either to marriage or to the episcopacy. In all three groups I detect a sense of tiredness about the discussion as people go round and round the exegetical uncertainties about the key passages. Some of these problems are intractable and it seems unlikely that further information will emerge to resolve them conclusively. There are quite a number within the evangelical constituency who find it genuinely difficult to make up their minds. Those who tried to predict the outcome of the 1992 synod vote on the ordination of women were frustrated by the size of the evangelical floating vote.

Inclusive language – is God male?

One issue which has injected some new fire into the debate recently is the question of inclusive language in relation to God. Evangelicals leap to attack a trend that appears to be departing from the text of Scripture, especially the naming of God as 'Father', a hallmark of Jesus's teaching and example in prayer. But in mounting a spirited defence against this it has proved to be dangerously easy to slip into an argument that identifies God as male. The issue has been well discussed by Hayter in *New Eve in Christ*. She notes the hostility throughout the biblical texts to 'the goddess' but sees it in parallel to hostility to the masculine Baal. The sexuality of both is linked to fertility rites and worship which is sexually promiscuous. God as 'Father' in the Old Testament occurs as a metaphor rather than a title, and there are mother metaphors as well. Our hopes and experience of parenting from both sexes contribute to our understanding of a relationship of love and trust and dependence on God. Jesus makes that transfer more immediate and direct with the encouragement to call God, 'Abba'. He does not thereby rule out motherly attributes of God and he uses a woman in a parable to image God (Luke 15.8–10).

Exploring this issue may prove to be fruitful for evangelical Anglicans if it encourages them to think more deeply about male and female and the sexuality which binds them so deeply together in community. There has been a tendency in the movement to undervalue the visual, the affective, the narrative and relational aspects of human thought, all the activities which we now know to be associated with the right hemisphere of the brain, which is half the Creator's gift to each human individual. Men and women working well together tend to correct the bias which creeps in when the sexes are isolated. In a fallen world there will always be pain associated with contact with the sexual 'other'. Apart, we are able to build defensive walls. Together, in Christ, they are torn down in his redeeming act of sacrificing love.

145

Notes

1. C. Gilligan, *In a Different Voice* (Cambridge, MA: Harvard University Press, 1982).
2. See M. S. van Leeuwen, *Gender and Grace: Women and Men in a Changing World* (Leicester: Inter-Varsity Press, 1990).
3. R. T. Beckwith, 'Ordination of Women: An Evangelical View' (Latimer Comment 29, Oxford, 1990).
4. Vera Sinton, 'Evangelical Social Ethics: Has it Betrayed the Gospel?' in M. Tinker, ed., *Restoring the Vision* (Eastbourne: Monarch, 1990).
5. For a fuller discussion see G. D. Fee, *The First Epistle to the Corinthians* (Grand Rapids, MI: Eerdmans, 1987).
6. D. Atkinson, *The Message of Genesis 1–11* (Leicester: Inter-Varsity Press, 1990).
7. A Statement by the House of Bishops of the General Synod of the Church of England, *Issues in Human Sexuality* (London: Church House Publishing, 1991), p. 7.
8. M. Hayter, *New Eve in Christ* (London: SPCK, 1987).
9. E. Storkey, *What's Right with Feminism* (London: SPCK, 1985); Kathy Keay, ed., *Men, Women and God* (London: Marshall Pickering, 1987).

12

Evangelicalism and Pastoral Ministry

DAVID ATKINSON

Pastoral theology

Pastoral theology has not traditionally been a very strong card in the evangelical Anglican pack. Before exploring why and illustrating how things are beginning to change, we shall first outline how 'pastoral theology' is understood in a context broader than the evangelical Anglican tradition.

The term 'pastoral theology' was not used until about 1750, although theology has always been understood to include a pastoral and practical dimension.[1] Many of the New Testament and patristic writings are pastorally directed. In the mid-nineteenth century, a particular trend in 'practical theology' emerged. Schleiermacher analysed theology into philosophical (the root), historical (the body) and practical (the crown) components. 'Practical theology' studied the means by which the community of faith preserves and protects its identity. 'Pastoral theology' was that aspect of practical theology concerned with the care of souls, focused largely on the homiletic and sacramental functions of priesthood. Schleiermacher's drawing of theology from the study of ministerial practice contrasts with that, for example, of J. J. van Oosterzee's *Practical Theology* (1878), where pastoral theology is understood as the application of doctrine to practice. In recent decades, especially in America, new styles of pastoral theology have arisen, largely inspired by Anton Boisen's reflections on a period of mental breakdown in his own life in *The Exploration of the Inner World* (1936). Boisen advocated a case-study method, integrating psychological and religious insights in his theological reflection on the 'human document'. He made a major impact on Seward Hiltner, one of several holders of newly-established professorships in the pastoral field in post-war America (others were Paul Johnson, Carroll Wise and Wayne Oates), and whose *Preface to Pastoral Theology* (1958) is regarded as a seminal text. Hiltner defined pastoral theology as 'that branch or field of theological knowledge and inquiry that brings the shepherding perspective to bear upon all operations and functions of the church and minister, and then draws conclusions of a theological order from reflection on these observations.'[2] It is an 'operation-centred' rather than a 'logic-centred' branch of theology primarily concerned with 'healing, sustaining and guiding'. It is not merely practice, nor applied doctrine, not pastoral psychology, nor only the theology of ministerial function. Although criticized for over-emphasising the rural metaphor of 'shepherd', and for promoting a professionalized view of clerical ministry which marginalized the laity, Hiltner contributed substantially to the 'reflective practitioner' model of pastoral theology.

Since Hiltner, several strands of pastoral theological enquiry have opened up. In the US, Wayne Oates wrote extensively on the theology of pastoral care in *Pastoral Counseling*, and several other titles. In *The Moral Context of Pastoral Care* Don Browning argued for a recovery of the moral dimension to pastoral care which, he feared, had become over-influenced by clinical psychologies. Browning edits the Fortress Press series of books on pastoral theology and has himself developed a *Fundamental Practical Theology* (1952), in which he reframes all theology in the light of the recent re-emergence of 'practical reasoning'. Donald Capps has explored the use of the Bible in pastoral care in his books *Pastoral Care and Hermeneutics* (1984) and *Reframing* (1990). Thomas Oden, having earlier written on the dialogue between theology and psychology in *Kerygma and Counselling* (1978), has recently produced a major *Pastoral Theology* (1983), concentrating on ministerial function, which draws on the classical Christian tradition – not least the patristic period.

Pastoral theology has had a lower profile elsewhere in the world. On the continent, Eduard Thurneysen wrote *A Theology of Pastoral Care* (1962) from a Barthian perspective, understanding pastoral care as part of proclamation of the Word of God. In London, Martyn Lloyd-Jones's expository preaching was essentially a proclamatory pastoral theology (see, for instance, his sermons on *Romans*, published during the 70s). In Switzerland, Paul Tournier[3] and Theodore Bovet[4] both worked at the interface between Christian faith and modern psychology. In England, missionary and psychiatrist Frank Lake, influenced by Object Relations theory, founded the Clinical Theology Association in 1962, and published his massive, if idiosyncratic, *Clinical Theology* in 1966. This developed a 'Christocentric' model of 'the dynamic cycle' of personal and spiritual development. In Birmingham, general practitioner, theologian and psychiatrist Bob Lambourne drew together Christian theology with medical and psychiatric practice.[5] In Holland, Jacob Firet constructed a theological model of pastoral role-fulfilment in *Dynamics of Pastoring* (1986). Alistair Campbell has written on the 'rediscovery of pastoral care' and the professional significance of pastoral ministry.[6] The SPCK New Library of Pastoral Care was planned to meet the needs of pastoral carers seeking to improve their knowledge and skills. These books are marked by careful use of contemporary secular psychotherapeutic knowledge, but less so for their theological perspectives, and have been criticized by some evangelicals for merely 'baptizing secular therapies'.

Much contemporary pastoral theology follows the 'reflective practitioner' model, in which theology arises out of reflection on pastoral practice.[7]

By contrast, evangelical theology has tended to be systematic and structured, rather than reflective and inductive. Some evangelicals tend to view much contemporary pastoral theology as too pragmatic, and not very 'theological' at all. The anxiety is that if the pastoral situation is allowed the guiding role in setting the theological agenda, the distinctive themes of the evangelical gospel may be diluted or lost. However, there is still a task to be undertaken in establishing a biblically rooted evangelical pastoral theology which recognizes the inescapably contextualized and practical nature of all theological enquiry.

Evangelical pastoral care: a recent rediscovery?

We said that pastoral theology has not been a very strong card in the evangelical Anglican pack. A brief glance at some British evangelical publications of the last three decades will illustrate this. Whether we look at the 1960s Christian Foundations Series,[8] or the Latimer Day Lectures of the Fellowship of Evangelical Churchmen, whether at the publications from Latimer House or from the Church Pastoral Aid Society, whether at John Stott's *One People* (1969), or Michael Harper's *Let My People Grow* (1977), whether at the *Guidelines* published before the Keele Congress in 1967, or the preparatory books for Nottingham NEAC in 1977, there is much discussion of 'ministry' in relation to church order, ordination, episcopacy and preaching, but very little pastoral theology. John King's *Evangelicals Today* (1973) has nothing on ministry or pastoral care, nor (apart from a few lines) does *Restoring the Vision* (ed. Melvin Tinker) published after the 1988 NEAC.

From the high-profile evangelical Anglican authors, there has been little concentration on the theology and practice of pastoral care and no developed systematic practical and pastoral theology. Their concerns have been elsewhere, no doubt in part due to the dominant priority in the 1960s and 70s of establishing evangelical identity as properly and appropriately both intelligent and Anglican.

This is not to say that pastoral care was not being exercised in many and effective ways. It is to say that it was not being written about very much. However, the strong if somewhat embattled loyalty to the evangelical cause of a previous generation seems now to have given way to a confidence from which other important concerns can be addressed. For at a lower-profile level, things have been changing.

The last two decades have seen the growth within evangelical Anglican theological colleges of more serious attention to pastoral theology, pastoral training, placement supervision, and critical theological reflection on pastoral practice. In part through the influence of Frank Lake, much pastoral training developed a therapeutic model of pastoral care, and began courses in pastoral counselling. More recently, colleges have placed this rather narrow therapeutic model of pastoral care within a broader theology of Christian ministry and mission. Some colleges offer diplomas or degrees in pastoral studies. One entire volume of *Anvil* in 1989[9] was given to pastoral theology. Evangelicals contributed to the symposium edited by Paul Ballard, *The Foundations of Pastoral Studies and Practical Theology* (1986). Dr Roger Hurding has written extensively on pastoral counselling in books which have achieved international acclaim.[10] Pastoral studies is no longer the Cinderella subject on the syllabus. Indeed, some teachers see their department as the hub, the focus for interdisciplinary discussion and exploration where biblical studies, doctrine, history, ethics, spirituality and worship can all come together; where the systematic and 'doxological' theological tasks of exploration and prayer meet the 'practical' theological tasks of ministry, mission and service.

In 1980, the Grove Booklets on Ministry and Worship were divided into the Grove Pastoral Series and the Grove Worship Series. The former included contributions on counselling and group work,[11] which began to open up the theology and practice of pastoral care, mostly expressed in terms of a therapeutic model. A further development of the therapeutic approach was the establishment in 1975 of *Care and Counsel*, initially at an evangelical Anglican church, though eventually becoming inter-denominational. This organization was set up to bring together the insights of biblical theology and professional therapy by offering a counselling service, training courses, a study group involving psychiatric, therapeutic, theological and pastoral expertise, and a series of biennial conferences for pastoral carers. There are similar agencies now in Bristol, Oxford, Cambridge, Nottingham and elsewhere.

Largely since Keele, evangelical Anglicans have also been rediscovering their social conscience, and their commitment to a transformative involvement in, rather than a pietistic withdrawal from, the world. Spurred on by the writings of Francis Schaeffer in the 1960s and 1970s in the history of ideas (though many evangelicals would want to move beyond Schaeffer); inspired by evangelical leaders such as Norman Anderson, bringing a Christian mind into the public realm; finding a new confidence in the professional world of social work (the Social Workers' Christian Fellowship was founded in 1964), and so on, a series of socially directed evangelical initiatives was begun. Study groups on race relations, medical ethics, justice and peace, family and sexual ethics, more recently on the environment, were started. The teaching of ethics and social theology were taken more seriously. The Grove Booklets on Ethics found a ready market. The certainty grew that if there is no social gospel, there is no gospel at all. With the growth of numbers of evangelical Anglicans in positions of prominence in the institutions of the state (politics, the civil service, the legal profession, education), and indeed within the Anglican church, the social and political dimensions to pastoral ministry and the theology of pastoral care have received new emphasis.

The beginnings, therefore, of an evangelical pastoral theology are underway. But there is a long road ahead.

The roots of evangelical pastoral care

If we are to develop an adequate evangelical theology of pastoral care, we must do so in relation to the ongoing evangelical tradition within the Anglican churches. Evangelical Anglicans have tended to look for inspiration in their thought and practice to several sources.

One source was the theology of the Reformation and some strands in the theology of the Puritans. The BCP Ordinal charges deacons to instruct the young, baptize, preach, visit the sick and the poor, and charges priests to be 'messengers, watchmen and stewards of the Lord', to teach, warn, feed and provide for the Lord's family, to seek for Christ's sheep that are dispersed abroad.

The Anglican priest turned reluctant non-conformist, Richard Baxter, whose *Reformed Pastor* (1656) set out a programme for parochial evangelism and catechesis, was another inspiration. This Reformation and Puritan focus on the ordained ministerial functions of preaching, teaching and pastoral visitation, have had a marked effect on evangelical approaches to ministry.

A second source of evangelical Anglican identity was the cross-centred spirituality, evangelistic heart and social concern of John and Charles Wesley in the eighteenth century. The Wesleys provided a theology and hymnody of evangelical piety, linked to an emphasis on evangelistic preaching, the personal experience of salvation, the quest for growth in personal holiness, and the development of small groups for nurturing faith and discipleship. The pastoral care shown by an older to a younger Christian in such nurture groups, the provision of devotional literature, Bible

152

study notes, and books of prayers and hymns, all formed part of ongoing evangelical spirituality.

The wise and balanced churchmanship of Charles Simeon (1759–1836) (though regarded by some as limiting and limited, certainly in relation to the social questions of his day), provides a third evangelical reference point.[12] Simeon was a noted preacher and pastor in Cambridge. He aimed at teaching 'scriptural divinity', refusing to be drawn into party dissension. His views were worked out in relation to his understanding of Scripture, and his sensitivity to the pastoral needs of his flock. His writings on contentious doctrines all have a pastoral dimension. Doctrine was to be lived, not just assented to. The central theme of all Scripture for Simeon was the cross of Christ; the means of conversion was the preaching of the gospel; faith was of no value if not attested by works. Simeon was involved in philanthropic public affairs, especially in provision for the poor, and in overseas missionary societies. His gospel involved social responsibility. He was a spiritual director, helping people to live a Christian life, and was personally involved in the ministry of counsel and encouragement. A strong and sacramental churchman, Simeon was a theologian – but of the pulpit rather than the lecture room.

A fourth source to which evangelical Anglicans turn was the social conscience of William Wilberforce seen in his work for the abolition of slavery, and of Lord Shaftesbury with his concern for justice in factory conditions, during last century. These significant social implications of the evangelical gospel have constantly reminded evangelical Anglicans (who have often forgotten it again) that the desire to be gospel people has an inescapable social component.

A fifth influence on contemporary evangelical Anglicans was the creative tension at the turn of this century between the Protestant,[13] rational, didactic, expository theology of J. C. Ryle, Bishop of Liverpool, and the perspectives on personal sanctification and spiritual experience of the Keswick Convention. A comparable tension is seen in different dress today in the discussions on Word and Spirit between those who stress the priority of preaching and rigorous, rational discipleship on the one hand, and the focus within the charismatic movement on broader gifts of ministry within the body of Christ, and a more emotional and celebratory tone of spirituality on the other.

More recent influences include contacts with contemporary American evangelicalism through evangelistic crusades and conferences, and the challenges posed to Anglican ecclesiology by the growing house church movement.

These influences are part of the evangelical Anglican identity from which a pastoral theology will grow. It is strong on teaching and personal discipleship, weaker on the church as a community of character; strong on grace and redemption; weaker on creation and incarnational theology.[14]

Five models of pastoral practice

Turning again to the contemporary scene, we need to enquire how evangelical pastoral care is actually practised. There seem to be five current models.

The proclamation and teaching model. For many evangelicals, the primary task of Christian ministry is the proclamation of the gospel. Frequently, proclamation is identified with expository preaching, teaching and verbal evangelism, and understood as the primary means of exercising pastoral care within a parochial setting. There is, clearly, a mode of preaching which can so bring the text of Scripture into touch with people's personal needs, that the Word of God strikes home in a powerfully life-changing way. It has to be said, however, that not all preaching is pastoral in this sense. Sometimes it is possible for the preacher precisely not to engage in pastoral ministry by hiding defensively behind the expository mode, ensuring that preaching is entirely cerebral and didactic in a way that fails to meet people where they are.

The nurture model. The pattern of discipleship learned in practice by many evangelical Anglican leaders has often included Christian summer training camps, university Christian Unions, local gatherings of like-minded clergy, Bible study groups and so on. With striking echoes of Wesley's class meetings, and the patterns of personal nurture in discipleship so developed, many evangelicals have learned their pastoral care by being nurtured and cared for

154

by an older like-minded Christian who has taken them under his (usually) wing, and taught them the faith, including most often a strong element of shared Bible study. This is a one-to-one, didactic approach to nurture. More recently, largely through the influence of the charismatic movement, 'fellowship groups' for shared worship, mutual support and sometimes for mutual therapy, have become the norm in many evangelical Anglican churches. This avoids the guru-mentality of the older model, but in its own way has sometimes developed hierarchies of 'shepherding' and authority which are not always liberating.

The service model. By 'service' is meant both that pastoral ministry which, motivated by compassion, emphasizes the importance of social welfare, and also the political commitment to social justice concerning the environments in which people live. Some evangelicals have stressed the former; some – particularly those in urban ministry – the latter. Some have combined both, with a growing realization that the quest for social justice is inescapably part of Christ's commission. Others have warned of the dangers of a social gospel which loses its evangelistic heart.

The therapy model. We have already noted that therapeutic models of pastoral care received a considerable impetus from the work of Frank Lake, and came to prominence in colleges and counselling agencies. Not all evangelicals were happy with the attempts of groups like *Care and Counsel* to marry biblical theology and the insights of secular human sciences. The unease may have been strengthened by an evangelical mistrust of the sort of 'natural theology' within which the human sciences have a place. Some feel more at home with the directive counselling of Jay Adams, who developed a 'nouthetic' approach[15] calling for repentance and a change of lifestyle informed by Scripture. Many others believe that Adams's approach shows too little sensitivity to human frailty and hurt, too little attention to God's gracious presence, too much emphasis on individual human responsibility for change, and an inappropriate use of the Bible. His 'proclamation' model of pastoral counselling is one extreme of a spectrum, at the other end of which are clinical theology and the other human relations-based models, developed in the Christian world, for example, by Michael Jacobs.[16]

Some evangelicals were tempted to think that pastoral care was

155

to be identified with pastoral counselling. But too narrow a focus on counselling can tend to the view that pastoral care is necessarily problem centred, whereas its concerns are more fully the whole of a person's life journey within the family and community; that pastoral care is necessarily individualistic, whereas human life and Christian fellowship are essentially corporate; that pastoral care is about relieving emotional pain, whereas the whole person in their physical, relational and spiritual dimensions must be part of the pastoral carer's concern. There has been some attempt to relate pastoral counselling to spiritual direction, and to healing ministry.

The mission model. Partly from dissatisfaction with the therapeutic model, some evangelical colleges have been developing models of pastoral care as part of the mission of the Christian church. Some evangelicals are more comfortable with 'mission' than with 'therapy' because it resonates with their historical involvement in missionary activity. However, the language of 'mission' needs to be handled carefully. Some want to press mission in pastoral care into the evangelistic terms of seeking individual conversion as the basis of pastoral ministry. Others, however, understand mission in a broader sense, as a sharing in the whole mission of Christ in the world, which of course includes evangelism. Mission, in the broad sense, is open to every working of God's 'common grace' in individuals and societies, and helps to give pastoral care a focus which is corporate rather than individualistic, Christ-centred rather than human need-centred, dynamic rather than static. In this sense, 'mission' may be a model which can hold together all that needs to be said about the homiletic, nurturing, serving and therapeutic aspects of pastoral care.

These different models within contemporary evangelical Anglicanism have led to approaches to pastoral ministry with different, sometimes conflicting, emphases. In practice, many pastors operate with varied models of ministry, each with fuzzy edges, sometimes with several at the same time, and without necessarily reflecting on what they are doing or why! As evangelical Anglicans have sought to affirm their place and commitment within broader Anglicanism, and as the influence of the charismatic renewal movement has also been significant, especially in worship, styles of ministry and personal spirituality, these emphases have been further complicated and modified. The ongoing tensions between clerical and lay ministries and the meaning of ordination; between formal and spontaneous patterns of worship; between hierarchical and shared patterns of leadership; between an individual and a corporate focus for discipleship; between evangelistic proclamation and social action; between an emphasis on the priority of preaching, and the searching for and use of other modes of communication, all arise out of, and are expressions of, the various threads within evangelical history and identity which we have explored. And they all affect the practice of pastoral care today. What is lacking is an adequate contemporary biblically based practical and pastoral theology, within which these various threads can all be held, and evaluated, together. There is, of course, much contemporary evangelical writing which has a strong pastoral dimension. J. I. Packer's best seller *Knowing God* (1973) has a very strong pastoral tone. Tom Smail's writings are rich pastorally directed explorations of the doctrines of the Holy Spirit and God the Father.[17] Many of the *The Bible Speaks Today* series of biblical expositions published by Inter-Varsity Press are intended to provide contemporary application of biblical themes to personal and pastoral situations. And there are several approaches to pastoral counselling which make links between therapeutic skills and biblical insights. But what is still needed is an evangelical Anglican theology of pastoral ministry which does for our generation what R. C. Moberly's *Ministerial Priesthood* (1897) did for the Catholic tradition in his.

The task

The task for evangelical Anglicans in this area is thus to articulate a theology of pastoral ministry shaped by the gospel, but which engages appropriately with the insights of the human sciences without being controlled by them, and which recognizes the importance of reflective theology, drawing on but also putting questions to more systematic evangelical doctrine. The task is made difficult by an often unspoken mistrust of 'the world', understood to include the human sciences, and by a weak doctrine of creation in comparison with the strong evangelical doctrines of grace and redemption. The task is also made harder by the lack of a substantial evangelical ecclesiology, which enables doctrinal and pastoral sense to be made of evangelical participation in the Anglican churches. Often such participation is made on pragmatic and pastoral grounds rather than on adequately justified historical and theological ones. What is needed is a theology of pastoral ministry integrally related to an evangelical Anglican ecclesiology.

The task would involve bringing the various models of pastoral practice into critical conversation with biblically rooted doctrine. It might begin with the doctrine of the Holy Trinity as persons in relation. It would explore the ministry of Christ from, and with, and to the Father in the power of the Spirit for the sake of the world. From this could develop a model of Christian ministry as the participation of the body of Christ in the ministry of Christ. It would have a 'gospel shape', grounded first of all in the grace of Christ, his incarnation, cross and resurrection, reaffirming God's creation, and pointing towards the kingdom of his glory. It would be grounded, secondly, in the love of God, which casts out fear, enabling people to face the truth which sets free, and which facilitates the growth of love and responsibility in people and in communities through forgiveness; a love, the social expression of which is justice. It would be grounded, thirdly, in the fellowship of the Holy Spirit, whose parakletic ministry, stretching from comfort to confrontation, from listening to spiritual direction, from liberating and healing to sacrificial service, is expressed ecclesially through the grace of the ascended Christ for his body in gifts of ministries, and not least through Word and sacrament. It would describe a ministry of proclamation and nurture, of service and healing, of justice and peace, rooted in this world order, but with an eschatological hope. It would express a ministry which is caught up into the ministry and mission of God to reconcile to himself all things in heaven and earth.

But that will need another essay, another time.

Notes

1. For much of this section I am indebted to J. N. Lapsely, 'Pastoral Theology, Past and Present' in Wm. B. Oglesby Jr, ed., *The New Shape*

of Pastoral Theology (Nashville, TN: Abingdon, 1969). See also K. E. Kirk, *The Vision of God* (London: Longmans, 1932), J. T. McNeil, *A history of the Cure of Souls* (New York: Harper & Row, 1951), W. A. Clebsch and C. Jaekle, *Pastoral Care in Historical Perspective* (Northvale, NJ: Aronson, 1975), M. Thornton, *English Spirituality* (London: SPCK, 1963).

2. S. Hiltner, *Preface to Pastoral Theology* (Nashville, TN: Abingdon, 1958), p. 20.

3. e.g. P. Tournier, *Guilt and Grace* (London: Hodder & Stoughton, 1962) and many other titles.

4. T. Bovet, *That They May Have Life* (London: Darton, Longman & Todd, tr. 1964).

5. R. A. Lambourne, *Community, Church and Healing* (London: Darton, Longman & Todd, 1963); *Explorations in Health and Salvation*, Institute for the Study of Worship and Religious Architecture (University of Birmingham, 1985).

6. e.g. A. Campbell, *Rediscovering Pastoral Care* (London: Darton, Longman & Todd, 1981); *Paid to Care?* (London: SPCK, 1985).

7. Cf. J. Patton, *From Ministry to Theology* (Nashville, TN: Abingdon, 1990), but contrast G. Leonard, *God Alive: Priorities in Pastoral Theology* (London: Darton, Longman & Todd, 1981).

8. e.g. J. R. W. Stott, *Confess Your Sins* (London: Hodder & Stoughton, 1964); M. Green, *Called to Serve* (London: Hodder & Stoughton, 1964).

9. Vol. 6, No. 3, 1989.

10. See especially R. Hurding, *Roots and Shoots* (London: Hodder & Stoughton, 1985).

11. e.g. R. Inwood, *Biblical Perspectives on Counselling*; R. Fowke, *Beginning Pastoral Counselling*.

12. See D. Webster, 'Simeon's Pastoral Theology' in A. Pollard and M. Hennell, ed., *Charles Simeon 1759–1836* (London: SPCK, 1964).

13. See J. C. Ryle, *Holiness* (Cambridge: James Clarke, 1952; rev. edn Welwyn, Herts: Evangelical Press, 1979).

14. Although there has been recent welcome evangelical interest in the pastoral theology of the Carolines, e.g., D. A. Scott, *Christian Character: Jeremy Taylor and Christian Ethics Today* (Oxford: Latimer House, 1991).

15. From the Greek *noutheteo*, to warn; see J. E. Adams, *Competent to Counsel* (Grand Rapids, MI: Baker Book House, 1970).

16. e.g. M. Jacobs, *Still Small Voice* (London: SPCK, 1982); *Towards the Fullness of Christ* (London: Darton, Longman & Todd, 1988).

17. T. A. Smail, *Reflected Glory* (London: Hodder & Stoughton, 1975); *The Forgotten Father* (London: Hodder & Stoughton, 1980).

13
Evangelicalism and Patterns of Ministry

GILLIAN SUMNER

It is a truism to say that the Anglican churches have no coherent understanding of ministry in general and ordination in particular. In recent years there has, however, been a growing convergence of understanding on a point of major significance: the ordained minister is no longer regarded primarily as the professional who runs the church, but rather as someone who makes a particular and significant contribution to the ministry of the whole *laos* (people) of God within the local church and community. 'The priesthood of all believers' is now seen less as a Protestant anti-clerical war cry and more as a statement about the corporate nature of priestly ministry – what it means, in fact, for the church to be the body of Christ, each member making a vital contribution to the whole.

To some extent this convergence has masked continuing theological differences about the nature of ordination and hence the nature of the distinctive contribution made by the ordained minister. It is a cause for great thankfulness that the evangelical and catholic wings of the church are increasingly discovering major areas of agreement, enabling them to go forward together in witness to the gospel. But ignoring their differences on the subject of ministry, however well intentioned in the interests of a united stand for the historic faith of the church, is bound to lead to friction and misunderstandings in the long term. Discerning and explaining the differences can lead to mutual understanding and respect.

The ordained ministry

According to the 'ontological' view of priesthood, the priest[1] is both to church and world an *alter Christus*. Ordination, together with the vocation and 'formation' which precede it, confers upon the priest an order of being which differs from that of the laity. He thus by his very presence contributes a sacramental dimension to the ministry of the whole *laos* of God, regardless of the functions he performs – although it receives visible and tangible expression in the liturgical sacraments and especially in the celebration of the eucharist.

Most evangelicals, on the other hand, still subscribe to a generally 'functional' view of ordained ministry. Any ministerial role within the body of Christ can, theologically speaking, be carried out by any lay member. The ordained minister is one in whom gifts of leadership have been discerned locally and tested by the wider church, who believes himself or herself to be called by God to this task, who has received appropriate training and is then duly authorized to exercise gifts of teaching and enabling others. Presidency at the eucharist, at present restricted by canon to the ordained priest, is an entirely suitable liturgical expression of this role; but for many, lay presidency would also be perfectly acceptable, where shared leadership of the local congregation made this appropriate.

Both 'wings' emphasize the quality of life of the ordained minister as indispensable, seeing growth in holiness and development of spirituality as essential to the leader who teaches by example, and integral to the sacramental 'character' of the priestly vocation. Both can therefore talk about 'ministerial formation'. Similarly, both wings recognize the ordained minister as 'representing' the church in the world. For evangelicals this may be simply a matter of recognizing that in public perceptions the vicar stands for the church. For the Catholic end of the spectrum, the priest is in himself a sacramental presence. 'Ministerial formation' and 'the minister as representative' are phrases also widely used by those who would describe themselves as holding the middle ground theologically. It is important to realize that common terminology is being used for a broad spectrum of content and expectations.

161

Evangelicals have not been immune from the general perception of the ordained clergyman as the professional among amateurs.[2] As the status of that profession has declined in society at large, so the perceived role of the clergyman has changed from that of an authority figure in the local church and community to that of a service provider – in more senses than one. This perception accords well with the value placed on service industries. In many ways the current emphasis in pastoral care on holistic understanding of the needs of an individual or group has coincided with similar emphases in health and social provision, combining to make the role of the vicar ancillary to the statutory services and local voluntary organizations. It also appears to sit very comfortably alongside the servanthood emphases of incarnational theology, and the description of the ordained minister as representative of the servant church.

In practice, however, most church traditions are expressing unease about the identification of the ordained minister as a social worker or counsellor with a bolt-on spiritual dimension. The tensions are felt particularly sharply by evangelicals, who have sought to maintain the primary New Testament emphasis on the presbyter as teacher, and many are wanting to reassert this priority. But all clergy have faced the pressures of increased expectations and reduced manpower. In a large eclectic town church or a multiple rural benefice, it has plainly become an impossibility for this comprehensive job description to be filled by any single individual of less than archangel status.

Collaborative ministry and patterns of leadership

For many in the Church of England, collaborative ministry is one of those slogans produced by hard-pressed bishops to make a virtue out of unpalatable necessity. Speaking of the ministry of the whole people of God is a high sounding way of saying we are short of clergy and funds to pay them, so if we want to keep the church going there will have to be some DIY.

In these circumstances, evangelicals have a contribution to make since they have, in theory, fewer theological inhibitions about disentangling themselves from accumulated traditional expectations, and their desire to return to New Testament principles of ministry is born of positive conviction rather than regrettable expediency. Across the years, evangelical Anglicans have accumulated a wide experience of a trained and biblically literate laity, committed to mutual pastoral care and to evangelism. They have evidence to convince others that it actually *works.* At their best, evangelicals have never lost sight of the New Testament understanding that the 'servant' role of the authorized church leader is to teach others and equip the whole body of Christ to be ministers of the gospel.

To establish foundational *principles* for ministry, evangelical Anglicans return to the pages of the New Testament; but there is a general consensus across all traditions (*pace* the Preface to the Ordinal) that the New Testament does not lay down any clear *pattern* of how those principles should work out in practice. Indeed, there is a great deal more guidance about potential pitfalls than about positive structures to be adopted. Nor is there encouragement in the New Testament to suppose that there should be any single ideal pattern which the church has only to work out and then set in concrete. The picture is one of development and change, risk and excitement. Even in the supposedly 'institutional-ized' church of the Pastoral Epistles, maturity and stability are needed because of undercurrents of dissent.

The scriptural principles which should undergird any pattern of ministerial leadership have been well summarized by Alec Motyer.[3] The specified functions of prebyters are teaching and oversight, 'companionate leadership'. Flexibility and plurality are the hallmarks of the New Testament leadership and structures: they emerge from within the local church in response to the needs of that particular community. The impression is not of a select élite, on a different plane from others, but of maturity and leading by example.

Belief in collaborative ministry has never been the sole prerogative of evangelical Anglicans. Throughout this century, where theologians and pastors and missionaries (facing a dilemma or even a crisis in ministerial strategy) have chosen to return to the New Testament, they have reached strikingly similar conclusions. In 1912, few would listen to the prophetic voice of Roland Allen, an Anglo-Catholic missionary in China, when he questioned the reliance of overseas missionary strategy on the ministry of the stipendiary expatriate priest.[4] In the years following Vatican II, Vincent Donovan practised as a Catholic priest among the Masai what Allen had advocated over fifty years earlier. He too underlined the relevance of his experiences to the church in the West, and has had considerable influence in the Anglican Communion.[5]

For evangelicals, however, the message is clear: a biblical concept of ministry they have always held dear has in recent years become fashionable (rather like the word evangelism). The church at large needs the secure base of a clearly articulated scriptural theology of ministry on which to build new collaborative patterns. The experience accumulated by evangelical churches over the years might save others from repeating mistakes or spending time reinventing the wheel. Evangelicals have the resources and the tradition from which to contribute to the current debate. It remains to be seen whether there is also the willingness to leave this contribution open-ended enough to accommodate the convictions of those from other traditions, while still maintaining scriptural essentials.

All this might seem to presuppose that evangelical Anglicans have practised what they preached. The reality has often been very different. Evangelicals have often gone along with the one-man-band, 'I am the professional among amateurs' view of the ordained minister; and 'incumbent in sole charge' is still an all too apt description of many evangelical vicars. Those who, by contrast, are most enthusiastic about shared ministry have often not thought through the principles or the consequences of their efforts and have succeeded in bringing chaos out of order instead of vice versa.

Some confusions

Within a rather muddled debate, certain particular sources of confusion can be identified.

First, the collaborative ministry of the whole people of God is often confused with collaborative leadership. There is no doubt that a church which claims to take seriously the complementary value of individual contributions within the body of Christ, and yet does not have shared leadership, must be viewed with suspicion. But there is a disturbing tendency to assume that developing each person's ministerial gifts means turning every

Christian into a leader, or at least setting their feet on a path which has becoming a leader as its ultimate goal.

Secondly, collaborative leadership itself is often confused with delegated responsibilities. The two are obviously interrelated but not by any means synonymous. Many harassed and overworked incumbents are only too glad to have a reader who will preach at regular intervals, or someone who will print and distribute the parish newsletter; but they are much less happy to allow the reader to initiate and co-ordinate mid-week groups or an editor to develop the form and content of all the church publicity. Giving real responsibility is an essential feature of sharing leadership. It is possible, however, to delegate responsibilities on the bicycle wheel model, spokes radiating out from the centre to the rim, but entirely held in place by the hub. The wheel is functional but inflexible, and if a few of the spokes become detached at either end, the whole wheel can be seriously damaged. If the hub is removed, the wheel structure collapses. Collaborative leadership needs a different model, based on the flexible and responsive interrelationships between those who carry different responsibilities.

A third source of confusion lies in the diaconate. There is a general agreement across the Anglican traditions that some very substantial theological and pastoral reflection needs to be done and that the position of women deacons as priests-in-waiting has confused the issue: now that this issue has been resolved, work can be done to give meaning to a permanent diaconate.[6] Meanwhile it has often been hard to find clarity for the distinctive roles of woman deacon, reader, lay pastoral assistant etc., and much depends on local practice. *The Deacon's Ministry,*[7] however, makes it plain that fundamental disagreements about the nature of ordination will again be raised. There is much in this book for evangelicals to learn; the writers, however, presuppose a predominantly catholic understanding of liturgical roles and of the sacramental nature of ordained ministry. Many of their suggestions would seem to an evangelical to belong to the representative functions of lay ministers. It could well be argued that a permanent diaconate (whether or not it continues to use that term) should subsume all forms of authorized lay ministry from wardens and parish administrators to readers and pastoral assistants.[8] *Diakonia* in the New Testament is not the prerogative of one particular group of office holders.

Non-stipendiary ministry

The very term 'non-stipendiary' starts with a negative connotation and suggests that the NSM is a substitute for the real thing. The common misconception is that NSMs are part-time, half-trained, and half-committed to ordained ministry.

Conventional wisdom about NSMs has gone in phases over the years. It has changed from viewing the 'auxiliary pastoral minister' as effectively an unpaid vicar's assistant, replacing the vanishing breed of curates, to believing that the focus of non-stipendiary ministry should be primarily in the place of work (the 'minister in secular employment'). Recently it has been more generally accepted that both work-focused and parish-focused roles are valid for NSMs.

Evangelicals have had numerous difficulties with the concept. Starting from verses like, 'The labourer is worthy of his hire' the assumption has gradually been made that all 'really professional' ministers should be paid – with all the inherent ambiguities of the word 'professional' left unresolved. Phrases such as 'He who puts his hand to the plough . . .' are left hanging in the air with the implication that those who remain in secular employment are unprepared for the financial sacrifices involved and not prepared to respond fully to the call of God. (Paul's own varying practice in this regard might challenge these assumptions.) Those retiring early are thought to be trying to have their material cake and eat it. Married women who want to work part-time cause particular difficulties. On the one hand the belief persists that it is the woman's job to make family life her priority, particularly while there are dependent children at home; on the other there is a desire to be positive about women's ministry and an increasing stress on the man's family responsibility. An agreement to work part-time is seen as somehow undermining the concept of total commitment.

There are also more fundamental theological reservations. As lay members of the church are given a high profile and increased responsibilities, as they lead family services, mid-week Bible study groups, baptism preparation and bereavement visiting teams, the question inevitably arises: What is the point of having part-time clergy in a parish when all the part-time functions can be carried out by lay people? Has ordination to non-stipendiary parochial ministry become simply a means of providing a spare pair of canonically acceptable eucharistic hands? In particular, as the Readers' Association stresses the role of a 'primarily teaching and preaching ministry within a pastoral context', there is often little to distinguish the regular ministry of an NSM from that of an able and active Reader. In many evangelical churches, NSMs have been sponsored for ordination by incumbents and congregations who wish to encourage the development of ministerial gifts; but the future role is undefined and after three years' demanding preparation, the NSM is effectively seen as a Reader who has done a bit more study. In other churches the NSM is a reserve on the touchline, brought into play to take baptisms and weddings when the vicar is ill or away, or when there is a clash of dates in a multiple benefice.

Evangelicals have had particular problems with the idea of the minister in secular employment. The theological rationale for MSE has traditionally emphasized the 'being' of the ordained priest in the workplace, contributing by his presence a sacramental dimension which complements but is significantly different from that of the lay Christian.[9] This view, however, relies upon the ontological view of priesthood. Evangelicals would wish to stress that the role of the ordained minister in the workplace does not differ in kind from that of any other lay Christian unless he or she has an official 'chaplaincy' role. Without this recognition, what is the point of ordination?

In practice, most MSEs without official status in their place of work find they are approached for pastoral help and guidance, receive requests for hospital visits in crises, are asked to take family weddings and funerals. Knowing them to be ordained, their fellow employees feel they have a measure of spiritual wisdom, can be trusted to preserve confidentiality, and can reasonably be asked for help. Yet they are more accessible to non-churchgoers than parish clergy because they are known as a workmate on the shop floor, a colleague in the school staff room.

But the MSE also has a particular responsibility to bring the challenges and needs of secular employment to the forefront of church concerns. Taking the New Testament seriously does not allow for privatized religion which opts out of the public domain. Yet increasingly overworked executives on the one hand, and workers frustrated by boredom or job uncertainty on the other, are understandably treating the local church as a weekend relaxation. Most training for MSE emphasizes theological reflection on the gospel and workplace. The MSE can thus become a catalyst for keeping faith and work issues high on the church agenda so that church life becomes a support base for discipleship at work, not a retreat from the hard realities of Monday morning. Similarly, parish-based NSMs not in secular employment can focus the attention of the church on local community concerns.

Clergy share ministerial functions in the church with lay people – Readers, Wardens, PCC officers and others who may not have official labels. If, as the New Testament suggests, presbyteral leadership is collegial, all *ordained* ministers share the responsibility for ministerial oversight. The purpose of ordination is to confirm the authorization of the wider church for this role of overseer (*episkopos*) within the leadership team. The question of stipendiary or non-stipendiary ministry thus becomes increasingly irrelevant, a matter of logistics and practicalities, rather than of the essential nature of ordained ministry.

Ordained women and styles of leadership

The experience of women in ordained ministry as deacons is of continuing significance even after the General Synod vote in November 1992.[10] Working collaboratively has been an essential feature of diaconal ministry for women. They have not been able to take total responsibility for the liturgical worship of their congregation nor to have sole control of a church's aims and activities – even had they wished to do so. In these circumstances, they have learned the value of collaboration in ministry – the enriching diversity of gifts and abilities, the mutual support between clerical colleagues and lay leaders. They have also experienced the frustrations of gifts ignored and ministry marginalized when the collaborative approach has been neglected, or more frequently when it has failed because it has not been properly carried through. They have been forced to analyse the causes of such failure, when good intentions have not been matched by skill in co-ordinating a collaborative team, or when ingrained habits of a dominant style have reasserted themselves. In all this, women deacons have shared the experience of many lay leaders, while yet themselves being clergy. They have thus been in effect a bridge.

At the institution of an incumbent, the bishop addresses the incumbent with the words, 'Receive this cure of souls which is both yours and mine.' Many incumbents find it very difficult to continue this process of delegated and shared pastoral responsibility with clergy colleagues, however experienced. As we have already noted, even incumbents who are ready to share their liturgical, teaching and administrative roles may feel that the weight of pastoral responsibility must fall on them alone. The ability of the ordained leaders to share vision, planning and prayer is often a mark of their ability to enable others to take real pastoral responsibility in shared ministry. Experienced women deacons have learned to appreciate this skill in incumbents where they have encountered it, and become very aware of the loss to the church where it is absent.

Even before the Church of England's decision to ordain women to the priesthood, a number of women deacons have already been ministers-in-charge of parishes and more will follow. This has given them the scope to initiate and develop patterns of collaborative ministry born out of long and sometimes painful experience.

The heart of the gospel shows God's strength made perfect in weakness and the Christian leader is called to exemplify this (2 Cor. 4.1–12). In our society admitting vulnerability is generally considered more acceptable for women than for men; and the particular experience of women deacons has often sharpened awareness of uncertainty, risk and rejection as well as the servanthood inherent in the diaconate. Women in ministry are considered by many to be 'more approachable' than their male colleagues, more realistic about living with pain, muddle and frustrations and therefore more likely to be understanding about emotional and practical stress. Whatever the truth underlying these public perceptions, women deacons would not wish the giving of added responsibility and status to carry with it a stereotype of invulnerability. Rather, they hope the process may free their male colleagues from the necessity of 'the clergy' always appearing to be strong and in control of every situation.

Many married clergymen have inherited a tradition that being ordained means sacrificing family life on the altar of parochial duty.[11] In recent years there has been some healthy questioning of this (often unspoken) assumption. However, these expectations are generally not extended to married women clergy. Particularly if they have children, it is expected that they will give a high priority to family life and that they will lead by example in this respect. As women become priests and incumbents, they would hope to retain this biblical perspective (cf. 1 Tim. 3.4–5; 12); and that the expectations of their male colleagues in this regard will be reassessed as a result. Similarly, it is generally (though sometimes belatedly) acknowledged that single women also need time for domestic commitments. Single male colleagues may benefit from a shift in perception about 'the clergy'.

The way these issues develop will have considerable repercussions for wider ministerial teams involving NSMs and lay leaders who have work and family commitments to be balanced alongside their pastoral responsibilities. Ordained women, whether priests or deacons, have a significant contribution to make.

Evangelical deployment

The majority of evangelical thinking on ecclesiology, ministry and evangelism is done against the background of large flourishing congregations in affluent middle class suburbia; and the next move is seen, often very commendably, as a 'church plant' in a new housing estate or revitalizing a church on the point of closure.

The evangelical constituency perhaps needs to recover its missionary vision and nerve. In recent decades, there has been a sea change in the relationship between the missionary societies supported by many evangelical churches and the indigenous church in the developing countries where those societies had traditionally worked. A new partnership has emerged, in which we in this country act as a support and resource for the church overseas; and at the same time, we have discovered that this is a two-way process – we have a lot to learn from them.

The potential now exists for similar partnerships on a wide scale in this country. With the increasing numbers of evangelical ordinands, more and more evangelical stipendiary clergy are finding themselves in livings of other traditions. They are discovering that, despite substantial difficulties, it *is* possible to contribute an evangelical theology and a biblical pastoral teaching ministry which seeks to enrich rather than to undermine other spiritualities. Similarly, non-stipendiary and reader ministries have been growth industries in recent years. Many large flourishing suburban churches have encouraged those with appropriate gifts to go forward for training – and then found themselves with a surfeit of potential preachers and service leaders sitting frustrated in the pews, while the incumbent nervously eyes the preaching roster and wonders whether he will ever be able to occupy the pulpit.

Some dioceses already deploy NSMs and, to a lesser extent, Readers to other parishes. If evangelical churches would view this less as 'X' being banished to a backwater – and more as a privileged opportunity for ministry, a strategy to be urged on their own dioceses,[12] they could make a very significant contribution. The difficulties, of course, are substantial. It is not easy to go from the lively worship of a large congregation with rich liturgical and musical resources and a tradition of expository sermons to an inner-city parish struggling for survival, or a small rural congregation. A solitary transplant can easily feel daunted, whilst too many becomes an intrusive invasion. There is no place for triumphant take-overs; this is collaborative ministry on a wider canvas. It need in no way stifle or deny the principles of local leadership and local ordained ministry. Realistically, such ministry often needs an outside catalyst.

The unwillingness of many stipendiary ordinands to look at parishes outside suburbia or north of Birmingham is often matched by the unwillingness of non-stipendiaries and Readers to move. In a mobile society, evangelicals tend either to buy a house on the basis that there is a 'good' church nearby or to buy first, then inspect the local church and worship elsewhere if it is found wanting. All of this is very understandable and there are no easy solutions, particularly when young families are involved. But the overall effect is to deplete the rural churches still further and deprive them of much-needed gifts. The tacit assumption is that a small congregation means a failed church – regardless of the fact that a congregation of twenty in a small village may mean a considerably higher proportion of churchgoers than 200 in a suburb, and that there are endless opportunities for Christians to build bridges in a village community. What is needed is for those who have experienced collaborative ministry and lay leadership to move outwards, working *with* the existing parochial framework, not to patronize or take over but to open up new possibilities.

With the emphasis on developing lay ministry, diocesan training has taken off in a big way in many places. Co-ordinators are often very open to evangelicals with proven teaching skills acting as tutors. Large evangelical Anglican churches have tended to aim at self-sufficiency in their teaching programme, again depriving the wider church of evangelical insights and leaving their own membership with very little understanding or appreciation of the rest of the Anglican church, its riches or its needs. This was understandable when the evangelical constituency felt itself to be a beleaguered minority guarding biblical truth, but its unquestioned continuance is yet another factor drawing evangelical Anglicans away from churches which do not have such teaching resources. The picture is changing, but slowly.

Conclusion

Evangelical Anglicans are frequently accused of 'not having an ecclesiology'. It would be more accurate to suggest that evangelicals have a well founded, scripturally based ecclesiology, but it has sometimes remained undeveloped – partly on account of a commitment to structures appropriate to the Reformation and partly on account of the pressure of years of being outnumbered and written off as 'fundamentalists'. The mentality of a minority under threat is always hard to eradicate; indeed, given the recent dramatic growth in numbers and acceptability of evangelicalism within Anglicanism, there is even the danger of a tendency to undergo a sudden metamorphosis and emerge as a form of triumphalism. Neither extreme is an adequate understanding of what it means to be part of such a varied institution as the Anglican church.

The corporate life of the gathered local church is a God-given provision for strengthening faith and love and prayer. The appropriate analogies for such fellowships are not, however, of the exclusive club or the jewel in a glass case, but of salt and light and

172

leaven, whose beneficial qualities are only effective when they permeate and become part of their surroundings. This is always a risky proceeding. Churches which develop patterns of ministry and of leadership equipped to take this risk become signs of the kingdom, of wholeness in Christ.

Notes

1. The term 'priest' is used advisedly. Both the catholic and the evangelical wings may find a role for the deacon in practice, but have difficulty forming an adequate theology for the diaconate. See below, p. 165.
2. A. Russell, *The Clerical Profession* (London: SPCK, 1984).
3. A. Motyer, 'The Meaning of Ministry' in M. Tinker, ed., *Restoring the Vision* (Eastbourne: MARC, 1990).
4. Relevant excerpts from Allen's writings are given in D. Paten and C. Long, eds, *The Compulsion of the Spirit* (Grand Rapids, MI: Eerdmans, 1983). Allen saw shared ministry primarily in terms of indigenous leaders emerging from each local congregation and being ordained. Current debates on Local Ordained Ministry reflect many of his concerns.
5. V. Donovan, *Christianity Rediscovered* (London: SCM Press, 1978). Some of the most radical reappraisals in recent years have come from the pen of Roman Catholic theologians. See for example the useful summary of Edward Schillebeeckx's views in J. Bowden, *Edward Schillebeeckx, Portrait of a Theologian* (London: SCM Press, 1983).
6. The Working Party report *Deacons Now* (London: ACCM, 1990), although it contains useful practical recommendations, has been essentially a holding operation.
7. C. Hall, ed., *The Deacon's Ministry* (London: Gracewing, 1981).
8. J. Tiller with M. Birchall, *The Gospel Community and its Leadership* (Basingstoke: Marshall, Morgan and Scott, 1987), goes a long way towards this conclusion.
9. *Ordained Ministry in Secular Employment*, ACCM Occasional paper 31 (London: ACCM, 1989).
10. These reflections owe much to a representative group of women deacons of the Oxford diocese, meeting before the Synod vote to discuss ways forward.
11. This tradition may have been due in part to the bishop's charge in the BCP ordinal, seeking to guard against lazy and absentee priests in a very different ecclesiastical context.
12. J. Tiller, *A Strategy for the Church's Ministry* (London: CIO, 1983). Tiller's recommendations, which had apparently sunk without trace, are now resurfacing in varying guises as diocesan strategies encounter financial pressures.

14

Evangelicalism:
An Outsider's Perspective

RICHARD HOLLOWAY

I have been asked to contribute an outsider's view on evangelicalism to this symposium and since I intend to fulfil the task by offering a somewhat critical perspective, let me begin with three major affirmations.

Since Christianity is a historical religion that fulfils its task by engaging with rather than withdrawing from human culture, it is in constant danger of so adapting itself to the context in which it is set as to dilute and neutralize its own nature and message. It becomes an echo, not a prophetic word, a benediction on the spirit of the age, rather than a challenge to it. There are complex issues in the relationship between Christianity and culture and the Christian movement has never had a single and prevailing response to the problem, but most historians of theology would admit that there has been and will probably remain a difficulty. It seems to me that, against this background, evangelicals at their best have maintained the 'otherness' of the Christian faith, what Paul Tillich called its heteronomous nature, in distinction to the rest of human culture. Many Christians who are at home in the world, with little sense of being strangers and exiles, far from their heavenly homeland, have little understanding of the revolutionary distinctiveness of the Christian faith. Evangelicals, on the other hand, are in no doubt about its distinctiveness. God in Christ has done a new thing and their passion is to bear witness to what God has done and continues to do in Christ.

Related to this conviction about the unique significance of Christian faith is the great evangelical conviction that being a

174

Christian makes a difference, or ought to make a difference, to the way we live. If Christ is a new creation and we are incorporated into Christ by baptism and grace then we, too, are called to newness of life. Evangelicals emphasize the contrast between the new and the old; they call Christians confidently to the life of conversion. Those of us who ask little of humanity in response to Christ receive little. Evangelicals ask for much and they often get it.

The third great characteristic of evangelicalism is its missionary energy. Christianity clearly began as a missionary religion, but much of that energy has been lost in Western Christianity. Many of us have too much fear of the kind of cultural imperialism that has used Christian mission as a cloak to be ourselves confident and effective evangelists. We become trapped in a kind of theological immobilism. Our hesitancy and uncertainty is in marked contrast to the energy and engagement of evangelicals. Their infectious zeal can be spectacularly successful in bringing people to Christ.

There is little doubt that much Western Christianity is cast in the role of residual beneficiary, living on the tail end of an inheritance from the past. Various versions of these residual forms of Christianity will doubtless persist for some time, but there can be little doubt that we are moving into a situation in which little knowledge of or sympathy for Christianity will be found in the population at large. If Christianity is to continue as a significant force in this new culture, therefore, it will have to recover something of the missionary energy that characterized the early church. It seems to be the case, so far, that only evangelical versions of Christianity are in possession of this energy. This certainly seems to be the case within the Anglican churches. It is entirely possible, therefore, that it is the evangelical version of Christianity that will survive and become dominant. This is why the publication of books like the present one is so important. If this is the future, let us see what it looks like. Just as importantly, if this is the future then let those of us who have anxieties about it declare them.

*   *   *

One of the most baffling things about Christianity is its multiformity. If we ignore the first nineteen hundred years of its history, a history of increasing complexity and multiplication, and study it only as a religious movement in the final years of the second millennium, it must strike the observer as multiform beyond all mending. It is estimated that there are at least 16,000 versions of Christianity in the world today and new forms are certainly coming into existence as these words are written. This complexity is undoubtedly evidence of the weakness and fallibility of historic Christianity, but it is also evidence of its enormous energy and dynamism. Anglicanism is only a sub-species of one version of historic Christianity but it is a significant one, mainly because it has, so far, managed to maintain a creative if uncomfortable multiformity within a fragile but distinctive unity. If Christian multiformity is both an actual weakness and a potential strength, then a form of Christianity that manages to maintain a significant diversity within a real unity has something to teach. I do not wish to rehearse the familiar outline of Anglican history, describing how we got to where we are, whether by accident or design, but I do wish to offer a positive interpretation of the phenomenon of Anglicanism, as an experience of Christianity that has a prophetic importance for a world that increasingly defines itself as pluralistic and post-confessional.

Two models suggest themselves to me as useful methods of interpreting Anglicanism. One of the lessons that we are slowly learning about our own planet is that it is an ecosystem in which a balanced diversity is intrinsic to its own nature and well-being. Distort or destroy this biodiversity and you damage and endanger the whole. That whole is a bewilderingly rich, minutely diversified system, in which differences are intrinsic to the health of everything, provided they balance and complement one another. The danger that faces the planet in our own time is due precisely to the distortions which the human species has inflicted upon the balance of the system. It would be possible, I believe, to interpret Anglicanism as a religious ecosystem in which the theological differences that characterize it are seen not as weaknesses, but as necessary aspects of the type of spiritual system we call a catholic church as opposed to a protestant sect; 'catholic' because it has an inclusivity and wholeness about it that allows a balanced multiplicity of expression and interpretation to exist within a single system. The danger that confronts sectarian versions of

Christianity is that they become unbalanced elements of a system with little sense of the larger reality; sectarians are usually incapable of seeing themselves in relation to the whole. This was precisely Paul's point in the letter to the Corinthians, when he likened the church to a body which was one reality with many members, and if the hand asserted itself against the eye and magnified its own function it distorted and endangered the life of the whole.

Another possible model for interpreting the phenomenon of Anglicanism comes from modern understandings of conflict control and the intellectual development of ideas. Conflict and the expression of difference are an essential part of truth seeking. It is often pointed out, for instance, that it is in the nature of a university not only to permit but to encourage debate and dissent in the search for truth, because truth itself is best served by this process. The dialectical theory of truth, which is a description or interpretation of actual human experience, shows us that a propositional truth is stated, a counter argument is postulated and the ensuing struggle between thesis and antithesis leads in time to a synthesis, a new level of truth that, as a result of the struggle between the previous two statements, transcends them. This, again, seems to me to be an appropriate model for the Christian community. Unless we are convinced that there is no virtue or significance in Christian diversity and see it only as evidence of humanity's proneness to error, the conflict model of truth seeking would seem to suggest that any community that cared for the truth would encourage and be open to theological struggle and diversity. Whether we like it or not, these are certainly the most conspicuous characteristics of historic Christianity.

Using these models, we can see that Anglicanism is a minor theological ecosystem in its own right or a permanent system of truth testing by conflict and disagreement. Historically, Anglicanism has emerged as an expression of Christianity that has continuities with both the pre-Reformation and the post-Reformation church. It stresses both the continuities and the discontinuities with pre-Reformation Catholicism. From the beginning, therefore, it has contained conservatives and radicals, though these terms have had varied import throughout its history. The dialectical nature of Anglicanism developed and evolved over the centuries as it continued its encounter with human history. Today Anglicanism can best be described as a dynamic continuum. Something of the same inclusiveness, though it is less celebrated or denigrated, characterizes the great Roman Catholic Church and many of the churches of the Reformation, but Anglican inclusiveness or comprehensiveness has become almost proverbial, some holding it as a badge of pride and others as a badge of contempt. However we interpret it, Anglicans describe a very wide continuum of practice and belief that is best diagramed as a broken circle that reaches from an extreme conservative evangelicalism on the left over to a conservative catholicism on the right, with innumerable subdivisions in between. It is one of the paradoxes of Anglicanism's broken circle that its extremes, though they are furthest from each other from one perspective, are closest from another. However, this figure does not quite capture the angularities and contrasts of Anglicanism. A better diagram would be the triangle, emphasizing the three points, evangelical, liberal and catholic, with various gradients between them. Some suggest that since there has been a further evolution in Anglican multiformity we must now include experiential or charismatic expressions of faith as a valid sub-type, leading to a square diagram. However we interpret it, configure it or justify it, Anglicanism is intrinsically pluriform and to be an intentional Anglican, as opposed to an incidental one, means to affirm the fact of this multiformity. To be an Anglican of any description involves acknowledging that the others are there. Even more than this seems to be called for. It is possible to offer a sort of grudging acknowledgment of the existence of other versions of Anglicanism without having any enthusiasm for them; but an intentional Anglican will seek not only to acknowledge, but to understand and affirm expressions of the common faith that may not be entirely sympathetic to his or her own tastes and convictions. Anglicanism may, in theory, be an ecosystem, but it can only be at its best if the different species interact and connect with one another. Historically this has not always happened and does not seem to be happening today. It is possible for Anglicans of particular persuasions to have little experience of other variations.

This is particularly true of the clergy. In the case of evangelicals, for instance, evangelical ordinands are drawn from evangelical parishes, trained at evangelical theological colleges, however broadly based they try to be, and probably sent to work, certainly in their first curacies, to evangelical parishes. This phenomenon can be innocent enough, but it can also lead to what is, in fact, a system of internal disaffiliation that comes close to schism, where particularly intentional versions of evangelicalism impose doctrinal tests or ecclesiastical embargoes on those within the same communion with whom they disagree. Those who have had anything to do with Christian organizations in universities know something of this phenomenon, whereby evangelical organizations impose on visiting speakers doctrinal tests in addition to the ones that, for instance, clergy have already passed on the road to ordination. Much of this, of course, is due to adolescent arrogance and intemperateness, but some of it is systemic to the evangelical experience. In certain of its forms there comes not only a celebration of its own effectiveness as a way of faith, but a rejection and negation of other expressions of the faith. Churches, in contrast to sectarian structures, are like other mature human communities, systems that balance contrarieties and disagreements in a way that enlarges and enriches the whole. Being in a church requires from us all an attitude of critical but genuine loyalty and a certain largeness of mind. Alan Paton said he became an Anglican because it was a church that affirmed more than it denied and he appreciated that generosity of mind and spirit. Is intentional evangelicalism consistent with intentional Anglicanism? Is intentional evangelicalism intrinsically sectarian or is it capable of the compromises of a mature ecclesiology? Is evangelical Anglicanism an internalized schism or a genuine variant within the Anglican experience? These questions have been addressed already in this book and evangelical Anglicans would answer them in different ways, but we know that some evangelicals in their arrogant dismissal of other Christian styles are the obverse of the Anglo-Papal absurdists within Anglicanism who claim both loyalty to the Holy See and membership of a church that defined itself historically by separating from Rome. Extreme versions of any variant within Anglicanism often end up by defining themselves as being in a state of internal disaffiliation, 'in' but not 'of' the body from which they claim the benefits of membership. Extreme Anglo-Catholics do it by dismissing most other Anglicans as being no longer members of the Catholic church. Extreme evangelicals do it by defining most other Anglicans as being no longer Christian. Leaders and expositors of each tradition in Anglicanism owe us the duty of repudiating such malevolent posturing.

* * *

Human beings seem to find it very difficult to live with complexity and difference. Social as well as intellectual history is bedevilled by the craving for single explanations of complex realities. There is a strong urge towards a theory of everything, an explanation into which we fit all the facts. The opposite of this monistic craving is what John Keats called 'negative capability', 'and that is when man is capable of being in uncertainties, Mysteries, doubts, without any irritable reaching after fact and reason'. In spite of the obvious complexity of theological history, including the complexities of the New Testament account of Jesus and the early church, Christians, like everyone else, seek to banish uncertainties and mysteries by the authority of clarity and definition. Christians are no worse at it than any other group of human beings; we find the same struggle towards a theory for everything as much in the scientific community as among the fundamentalist groups in all religious systems. This monistic trend in intellectual history, both secular and theological, is a particular characteristic of the West, in marked contrast to the traditions of the East. In her recent book *Science and the Soul* Angela Tilby has suggested that the mystical or apophatic tradition of Eastern Orthodoxy may be better placed to engage with the complexities of the new cosmology. She writes:

> Given the way in which science has now crowded out theology and made the doctrine of God's transcendence redundant, such an apophatic mystical approach might be appropriate for the recovery of a Christian picture of God in our age. A number of eminent scientists have been drawn to mysticism through the discoveries of the twentieth century.
>
> In the West there is an inexorable striving for a simple, unitary description of God. Western theology, under the influence of Aristotle, fuses the being of God with God's action. God is seen as the one who 'does' the universe. He is pure act. Where the West fuses God's being and God's act, the East insists that there is a distinction in what God is in his essence, and the

divine energies which manifest God's nature. There is room for complexity in the Eastern view of God. God is less monolithic and absolute in simplicity, and therefore more dynamic in relation to the world. The essence of God remains unknowable and incommunicable. But God overflows his essence in manifesting his presence in the energies, which bear the innumerable names of God, like wisdom, power, life, justice and love.[1]

The paradox of the present evangelical ascendance in an increasingly scientific and secular culture is that it might end up simply offering people an alternative theory of the universe, rather than a living experience of the mystery of God.

We see something of this same passion for single explanations in the evangelical preoccupation with the sin and redemption model of Christ's work. The sin and redemption model of God's action through Christ's atoning sacrifice is undoubtedly a powerful strand in the New Testament. It is interesting, however, that the Catholic Church has never defined the mystery of the atonement. It has, instead, following the New Testament itself, offered a series of metaphors to describe the Christian experience of salvation through Christ. Evangelicals, however, tend to make commitment to the substitutionary theory of atonement one of the prime tests of doctrinal purity. This is a good example of the evangelicals' lack of negative capability and their passion for interpretative theories that offer single explanations for complex realities.

Related to the evangelicals' firm hold on a specific theory of atonement is their slacker grip on the doctrines of creation and incarnation. These doctrines lay more stress on the continuities between God and humanity than on the discontinuities; the presence of God in history and culture rather than the gap between them; the intactness, however defaced, of the divine image in humanity rather than its destruction. The doctrines of creation and incarnation, of course, are the great Catholic doctrines. They have bred in Christianity, at its best, an affirming and generous attitude towards human beings, their struggles, their joys, their tragedies and their sorrows.

One consequence of this incarnational approach has been the emergence of a Christian aesthetic in worship, art and architecture. Because these are human realities they are, of course, flawed and can become inflated, even idolatrous. The evangelical tendency, on the other hand, is towards a sort of aesthetic contraction and banality in which liturgy is fast food rather than haute cuisine. We know there are solid missionary reasons for this liturgical reductionism. It makes worship accessible to people in a way that the more developed liturgies do not. More people go to discos than to high opera, and one of the courageous things about evangelicals is their ability to embrace bad taste for the sake of the gospel. Indeed, the Archbishop of Canterbury, himself a notable evangelical, has pointed out that the Church of England is in danger of dying of good taste. Nevertheless, there is a genuine problem here. The Christian life is a process of formation and sanctification, development is built into it. How much openness is there among evangelical Anglicans to appropriate liturgical development? How much sympathy, for instance, is there towards the evangelistic possibilities of the traditional Holy Week liturgies, not to mention the function of symbol and sacrament in the redeeming of time and the sanctification of the people of God? How much sense is there that *places* can become holy and mediate the divine, including churches that are prayed in on weekdays as well as weekends and where aids to prayer and devotion are offered to the soul in search of God? Have evangelicals, in fact, studied and understood the sanctifying possibilities of the Catholic spiritual tradition, or does their unipolar preoccupation with redemption theology blind them to the beautiful generosity of God in creation?

Finally, my most acute discomfort with evangelicalism is with its moralism. I am well aware of the social successes of Puritanism and its connection with the development of Western capitalism, but it is its very successes I fear. I am intrigued by the number of chief constables who seem to be card-carrying evangelicals. I know society needs its disciplinarians, but something in me shrinks from these successful, sober-suited authoritarians, who are convinced they have the answer to society's problems. Perhaps perversely, I am drawn to and feel more at ease with the wilder and more creative anti-puritans, because I find a deeper sympathy for the human condition among them than among history's chief constables. This may be due to my own moral sloppiness, but it is also a tendency I detect in Jesus Christ who was deeply suspected by the respectable disciplinarians of his day. I am haunted by a saying of Charles Peguy, 'The sinner is at the very heart of Christianity. No one understands Christianity better than the sinner. No one, unless it be the saint.' A church for sinners I can understand and welcome, particularly a church for sinners who long one day to be sanctified by the unconditional grace of God. But a church of the good and respectable I find mysteriously unappealing, maybe because I feel personally judged by such a group. What this is all about I cannot entirely explain (and it clearly has as much to do with my own weaknesses as with those of evangelicalism) but I set it down here because I do not believe I am untypical. Evangelicals make the rest of us feel not quite kosher, theologically and morally inadequate.

Related to this preoccupation with moral successfulness and theological purity is a cluster of other aspects of contemporary evangelicalism that seem to me to be symptoms of stress rather than free responses to the grace of God. The preoccupation with church planting, with congregational development often at the expense of depth, suggests the presence of an understanding of God that is still profoundly Pelagian, whereas the thing that is worth celebrating in the Christian gospel is that it is free. There is more than a whiff of justification by works in the energies and apparent competitiveness of some evangelical groups; and in their moralism, especially their preoccupation with sexual activity, there is a tendency to turn the gospel from grace to law, to give people the impression that their salvation is something they have to win for themselves, whereas the really good thing about Christianity, the thing that makes it *good* news, is that God saves us through Christ by grace. There may be no free lunches in the harsh disciplined culture of late twentieth-century Britain; but the messianic banquet is free; access to God is free; all the walls have been flattened. We do not, cannot, earn God's grace. It is poured out upon us abundantly, upon the righteous, the unrighteous, the sinner, the saint, the chief constable and the gay priest. 'Amazing Grace' used to be the great love song of evangelicalism. What happened to it?

Note

1. Angela Tilby, *Science and the Soul* (London: SPCK, 1992), p. 243.